★ OLYMPIC GUIDES ★

A BASIC GUIDE TO

Figure Skating

An Official U.S. Olympic Committee Sports Series

The U.S. Olympic Committee

Griffin Publishing Group

This Hardcover Edition Distributed By
Gareth Stevens Publishing
A World Almanac Education Group Company

This hardcover edition distributed by
Gareth Stevens Publishing
A World Almanac Education Group Company
330 West Olive Street, Suite 100
Milwaukee, WI 53212 USA
Please visit our web site at: www.garethstevens.com

For a free color catalog describing Gareth Stevens' list of high-quality books and multimedia programs, call 1-800-542-2595 or fax your request to (414) 332-3567.

Library of Congress Cataloging-in-Publication Data for this hardcover edition available upon request from Gareth Stevens Publishing. Fax (414) 336-0157 for the attention of the Publishing Records Department.

Hardcover edition: ISBN 0-8368-3102-0

Editorial Statement
In the interest of brevity, the Editors have chosen to use the standard English form of address. Please be advised that this usage is not meant to suggest a restriction to, nor an endorsement of, any individual or group of individuals, either by age, gender, or athletic ability. The Editors certainly acknowledge that boys and girls, men and women, of every age and physical condition are actively involved in sports, and we encourage everyone to enjoy the sports of his or her choice.

1 2 3 4 5 6 7 8 9 06 05 04 03 02
Printed in the United States of America

ACKNOWLEDGMENTS

PUBLISHER   **Griffin Publishing Group**

DIR. / OPERATIONS   **Robin L. Howland**

PROJECT MANAGER   **Bryan K. Howland**

WRITER   **Thomas Pickering**

BOOK DESIGN   **m2design group**

U.S. FIGURE SKATING ASSOCIATION

PRESIDENT   **Phyllis Howard**

EXECUTIVE DIRECTOR   **John F. LeFevre**

EDITOR   **Geoffrey M. Horn**

PHOTOS   **ALLSPORT**

COVER DESIGN   **m2design group**

COVER PHOTO   **Doug Pensinger/ALLSPORT**

ATHLETE ON COVER   **Michelle Kwan**

THE UNITED STATES OLYMPIC COMMITTEE

The U.S. Olympic Committee (USOC) is the custodian of the U.S. Olympic Movement and is dedicated to providing opportunities for American athletes of all ages.

The USOC, a streamlined organization of member organizations, is the moving force for support of sports in the United States that are on the program of the Olympic and/or Pan American Games, or those wishing to be included.

The USOC has been recognized by the International Olympic Committee since 1894 as the sole agency in the United States whose mission involves training, entering, and underwriting the full expenses for the United States teams in the Olympic and Pan American Games. The USOC also supports the bid of U.S. cities to host the winter and summer Olympic Games, or the winter and summer Pan American Games, and after reviewing all the candidates, votes on and may endorse one city per event as the U.S. bid city. The USOC also approves the U.S. trial sites for the Olympic and Pan American Games team selections.

WELCOME TO THE OLYMPIC SPORTS SERIES

We feel this unique series will encourage parents, athletes of all ages, and novices who are thinking about a sport for the first time to get involved with the challenging and rewarding world of Olympic sports.

This series of Olympic sport books covers both summer and winter sports, features Olympic history and basic sports fundamentals, and encourages family involvement. Each book includes information on how to get started in a particular sport, including equipment and clothing; rules of the game; health and fitness; basic first aid; and guidelines for spectators. Of special interest is the information on opportunities for senior citizens, volunteers, and physically challenged athletes. In addition, each book is enhanced by photographs and illustrations and a complete, easy-to-understand glossary.

Because this family-oriented series neither assumes nor requires prior knowledge of a particular sport, it can be enjoyed by all age groups. Regardless of anyone's level of sports knowledge, playing experience, or athletic ability, this official U.S. Olympic Committee Sports Series will encourage understanding and participation in sports and fitness.

The purchase of these books will assist the U.S. Olympic Team. This series supports the Olympic mission and serves importantly to enhance participation in the Olympic and Pan American Games.

United States Olympic Committee

Contents

U S A

AN ATHLETE'S CREED

The most important thing in the Olympic Games is not to win but to take part, just as the most important thing in life is not the triumph but the struggle. The essential thing is not to have conquered but to have fought well.

These famous words, commonly referred to as the Olympic Creed, were once spoken by Baron Pierre de Coubertin, founder of the modern Olympic Games. Whatever their origins, they aptly describe the theme behind each and every Olympic competition.

Metric Equivalents

Wherever possible, measurements given are those specified by the Olympic rules. Other measurements are given in metric or standard U.S. units, as appropriate. For purposes of comparison, the following rough equivalents may be used.

1 kilometer (km)	= 0.62 mile (mi)	1 mi = 1.61 km
1 meter (m)	= 3.28 feet (ft)	1 ft = 0.305 m
	= 1.09 yards (yd)	1 yd = 0.91 m
1 centimeter (cm)	= 0.39 inch (in)	1 in = 2.54 cm
	= 0.1 hand	1 hand (4 in) = 10.2 cm
1 kilogram (kg)	= 2.2 pounds (lb)	1 lb = 0.45 kg
1 milliliter (ml)	= 0.03 fluid ounce (fl oz)	1 fl oz = 29.573 ml
1 liter	= 0.26 gallons (gal)	1 gal = 3.785 liters

1

Figure Skating and the Olympics

Although skating did not appear in the Olympics until the London Games of 1908, its roots go back centuries.

While very old skates, probably dating to 3000 B.C., have been found in Switzerland, most historians agree that the first true skaters were from Finland. It's likely these first Scandinavian skaters used the bones of horses, elk, and reindeer to make blades, which they tied to shoe or boot bottoms to make traveling over ice easier and faster. Later, the blades were fastened, or clamped, onto shoes or boots, much like old-fashioned roller skates. Farther north, in Siberia and other Arctic areas, walrus tusks, which can be two feet long and weigh as much as eight pounds, were used for blades. When bones were not available, wood was used.

Skates changed forever with the introduction of iron blades in 1572. Iron skates helped skaters maintain forward motion and push ahead, while reducing friction and slipping. There were disadvantages to iron blades: they did not stay sharp for very long, and strapping or tying the blades to street shoes provided little or no ankle support. Nevertheless, iron skates were used until the next major development—steel blades—in the 1700s.

IOC /ALLSPORT

An ice skate from 1956

Skates with steel blades attached to a leather high-top boot supported the skater's ankle and made skating safer and more comfortable. It was with these "modern" skates that the sport boomed.

In the 1200s and 1300s, skaters in the Netherlands skated on frozen lakes and canals. These early skaters used long, sharp sticks to poke the ice and propel themselves, much as skiers do with ski poles. This technique made winter transportation much easier for the Dutch, who could skate from village to village on their frozen canals, but skating for recreation was a much later development. The Dutch pioneered the push-glide, push-glide motion all skaters use today. They called it the "Dutch roll." It was smoother and faster than the earlier method, and it allowed skaters to throw away their sharp sticks.

Across the North Sea, in the British Isles, the Scots were skating, too. In Edinburgh in 1683, Scottish skaters established the first skating club. The major requirement for admission was to be able to jump over three top hats lined up in a row! Skating also reached England in the 1700s, where it became an outdoor activity for aristocrats, as it had been on the European continent. Skaters in full-length dresses and suits and waistcoats glided on the ice in a formal, elegant style.

British colonists and Scottish immigrants brought the sport of skating to North America, but it did not become a popular outdoor winter activity right away. In 1876, artificial ice was first used in indoor rinks. This meant people could enjoy skating for exercise and recreation in any season, and the popularity of the sport grew from there.

The first skating organization in the United States was the Skating Club of the City and County of Philadelphia, founded in 1849. Twelve years later, it joined with the Humane Society to become the Philadelphia Skating Club and Humane Society. The "humane" part was needed because members carried ropes in order to rescue anyone who had fallen through the ice. (Rope carrying is no longer a requirement for membership!)

Origins of Figure Skating

IOC /ALLSPORT

1908 Games in London pairs skating competitors

The term "figure skating" was first used in England in the 1800s. The English had come to consider skating a science, and they began imposing rigid requirements on club skaters to carve patterns in the ice with their sharp blades. Eventually, this became a formal routine— the English Style—and the skaters competed by "drawing" or carving figures in the ice over and over.

The figure skating we see in today's Winter Olympic Games is a long way from those early figures carved by club skaters. For that, we can thank an American ballet dancer and skater, Jackson Haines, who revolutionized figure skating by freeing it from its formal, programmed style. Haines had learned English Style skating, but preferred a style that was like dancing to music on ice. He did everything on ice—leaps, spins, backbends—but he didn't do figures. Instead, his movements flowed and expressed emotion, often following the gliding steps of a popular dance, the waltz.

IOC /ALLSPORT

The ice rink for the 1936 Olympic Games
in Garmisch-Partenkirchen, Germany

Although he was American figure skating champion in 1863 and 1864, and the first to perform a "sit spin," Haines and his figure skating style were not popular in America. People laughed at him and stayed with traditional skating, repeatedly tracing and retracing the same patterns on ice. The British, like the Americans, didn't approve of Haines. But Europeans were enthusiastic imitators, and his popularity soared on the continent. In Vienna he gave "waltzing on ice" lessons and fathered the International Style of figure skating, which finally became popular in the United States in the early 1900s. Haines was the first to screw metal blades to the sole of a special "figure skating boot," giving him better support and control over his movements.

Early International Competitions

Figure skating became an official sport in the 1908 Olympic Games in London. It was at the London Games that the first American to participate in international competition, Irving Brokaw of Cambridge, Massachusetts, first used Haines's International Style in competition, finishing sixth.

The International Style of figure skating gained popularity with some skaters, while others stuck with the English Style. In an exhibition at the 1920 Games in Antwerp, Belgium, Theresa Weld of the United States became the first woman to perform a single "salchow" jump at a competition. For this breech of figure skating etiquette, she was reprimanded. In those days, jumping was not considered "proper" for young ladies.

The first winter version of the Olympic Games began on January 25, 1924, in Chamonix, France. Sixteen countries sent 258 athletes, including 13 women, to participate. There were 13 events, including four-man bobsled, ice hockey, figure skating, speed skating, and Nordic skiing and ski jumping.

Sonja Henie

IOC /ALLSPORT

Sonja Henie of Norway practices her routine for the 1928 Olympics in St. Moritz, Switzerland.

Europeans dominated figure skating at the early Winter Games. The most famous of these dominant European skaters was a Norwegian woman named Sonja Henie.

Sonja Henie was born on April 8, 1912, in Oslo, the capital of Norway. For her sixth birthday, she received her first skates, and her older brother taught her the basics of skating, from how to fall to how to figure skate in the classic English Style. Sonja took over from there, practicing until she was nearly perfect. It was said that her figures were so precise that she could trace the same

IOC /ALLSPORT

Karl Schaefer of Austria and
Sonja Henie of Norway
relax on the ice.

figure over and over and make it appear to be only one line!

Henie also took ballet lessons and loved to dance. So it seemed natural to her when she started combining dancing with ice skating.

In 1922, at age 10, Henie won the Norwegian women's figure skating title, and in 1924 she entered the first Winter Olympic Games. She was athletic and different, wearing a short dress that was daring for that era, and performing a jump. Jumps were still considered improper for young ladies, and Sonja finished last.

Rather than give up, Henie kept practicing her figures *and* her jumps. In the 1928 Winter Games, she won the first of three straight Olympic gold medals (1928, 1932, 1936). She also won ten straight World Championships (1927–1936). Those are records no other woman skater has been able to match.

Henie was the first international skating star to show the beauty of figure skating to the world. She combined music, choreography, and beautiful costumes with figure skating, and created a legacy as important as that of Haines. She was an immensely popular athlete who went on to produce ice shows and star in movies. Her figure skating achievements opened doors for thousands of youngsters all over the world.

American Figure Skaters

No other country has produced as many medal-winning champion skaters as the United States. Through the 1998 Games in Nagano, U.S. figure skaters had won 40 Olympic medals, including 12 gold medals. At the World Championships through 2000, 160 skaters from the United States had earned medals, 47 of them for the world title.

In the Winter Olympic Games between 1948 and 1960, figure skaters from the United States were outstanding. Led by Dick Button, the American men captured four gold medals in a row (1948–1960) in men's singles, plus one silver and two bronze

IOC /ALLSPORT

Dick Button, the first skater to perform a triple loop

medals. At the same time, American women led by Tenley Albright and Carol Heiss won two golds and two silver medals, and claimed nearly all of the World Championships.

Dick Button is credited with changing modern figure skating to its current athletic approach. With the possible exception of Sonja Henie, no one has had more of an impact on the sport than Button. He amazed crowds by performing unheard-of athletic feats—acrobatic leaps and spins—on ice skates.

Button's "firsts" included a double axel at the 1948 Winter Olympic Games and a triple loop at the 1952 Games. Button, who won five World Championships and two Olympic championships, also invented the so-called Button camel spin. His American Style made men's figure skating more athletic and more interesting to young men around the world.

In 1956 another American, Hayes Jenkins, won the Olympic gold medal for men's figure skating. Hayes, also a four-time winner of the Men's World Figure Skating Championships (1953–1956), was part of a famous brother team that dominated skating during the 1950s. David Jenkins picked up where Hayes left off, winning the World Championships in 1957, 1958, and 1959. David won the family's second Olympic gold medal in the 1960 Winter Games.

By any standard, Tenley Albright was an extraordinary Olympic performer. She overcame polio at the age of 11 to become a world-class figure skater and world-class medical scholar. While a full-time student at Harvard in 1953, she became the first woman figure skater from the United States to win a World Championship. Three years later, she became the first to win an Olympic gold medal, at the 1956 Winter Games in Cortina, Italy. Immediately after winning her Olympic title, Albright refocused her energy and entered Harvard Medical School, from which she graduated with honors to become a pioneer in cancer studies.

Carol Heiss, who was a silver medal winner at the Cortina Winter Games in 1956, became America's next great woman figure skater. Heiss won five straight World Championships from 1956 through 1960. She capped the year 1960 by also winning an Olympic gold medal.

By the 1960s, new skating stars with new skating styles were making news in the United States and at both the World Championships and the Olympic Games. Peggy Fleming was 15 in 1964 when she won the U.S. Figure Skating Championship in women's singles. She went on to win four more U.S. titles (1965–1968) and three World Championships (1966–1968).

Fleming was different, and so was her style of skating. She was not really muscular at all, but petite and slender. Also, she didn't attack her program, but skated with what appeared to be no effort at all. In 1968 she won the gold medal at the Olympic

IOC /ALLSPORT

Peggy Fleming of the USA skating in the
Olympic Games of 1968 in Grenoble, France

Winter Games in Grenoble, France, becoming the first skating champion to be seen worldwide on television via satellite. This brought instant fame to her and generated a booming interest in figure skating everywhere.

Tony Duffy /ALLSPORT

Three-time world champion Dorothy Hamill of the USA

By the 1976 Games at Innsbruck, Austria, the world television audience for the women's figure skating finals had grown to half a billion people. That was the year Dorothy Hamill, a three-time world champion, showed the world the "Hamill camel"—a camel spin that flowed into a sit spin. In a unanimous decision, Dorothy Hamill won the gold medal.

One of America's most colorful performers was 1984 Olympic gold medalist Scott Hamilton. He contracted an unusual illness as a small child that restricted his growth. Though Scott enjoyed the skating that helped him fit in with taller kids his own age, his adoptive parents had little money for lessons. His upbeat personality and drive to be a great skater caught the attention of some people in the community who offered to pay for his lessons. He was ultimately able to justify their faith in him by winning four straight World Championships (1981–1984) and the Olympic men's single's title in 1984.

In 1988 in Calgary, Alberta, Canada, Brian Boitano won gold in a spirited duel with Canada's Brian Orser. Boitano's gold was one of two the United States won that year.

Kristi Yamaguchi ended a 16-year hiatus for the United States in women's singles when she won the gold medal in 1992 at Albertville, France. Six years later, Tara Lipinski of the United States captured the gold at the Winter Games in Nagano, Japan, becoming, at 15, the youngest woman ever to win an Olympic figure-skating title.

Steve Powell/ALLSPORT

Scott Hamilton in the 1984 Olympics in Sarajevo, Yugoslavia

U.S. Figure Skating Champions
Women's Singles

1914	Theresa Weld	1940	Joan Tozzer
1915-17	No competitions	1941	Jane Vaughn
1918	Rosemary Beresford	1942	Jane Vaughn
1919	No competitions	1943	Gretchen Merrill
1920	Theresa Weld	1944	Gretchen Merrill
1921	Theresa Blanchard	1945	Gretchen Merrill
1922	Theresa Blanchard	1946	Gretchen Merrill
1923	Theresa Blanchard	1947	Gretchen Merrill
1924	Theresa Blanchard	1948	Gretchen Merrill
1925	Beatrix Loughran	1949	Yvonne C. Sherman
1926	Beatrix Loughran	1950	Yvonne C. Sherman
1927	Beatrix Loughran	1951	Sonya Klopfer
1928	Maribel Vinson	1952	Tenley Albright
1929	Maribel Vinson	1953	Tenley Albright
1930	Maribel Vinson	1954	Tenley Albright
1931	Maribel Vinson	1955	Tenley Albright
1932	Maribel Vinson	1956	Tenley Albright
1933	Maribel Vinson	1957	Carol Heiss
1934	Suzanne Davis	1958	Carol Heiss
1935	Maribel Vinson	1959	Carol Heiss
1936	Maribel Vinson	1960	Carol Heiss
1937	Maribel Vinson	1961	Laurence Owen
1938	Joan Tozzer	1962	Barbara Roles
1939	Joan Tozzer	1963	Lorraine Hanlon

1964	Peggy Fleming	1983	Rosalynn Sumners
1965	Peggy Fleming	1984	Rosalynn Sumners
1966	Peggy Fleming	1985	Tiffany Chin
1967	Peggy Fleming	1986	Debi Thomas
1968	Peggy Fleming	1987	Jill Trenary
1969	Janet Lynn	1988	Debi Thomas
1970	Janet Lynn	1989	Jill Trenary
1971	Janet Lynn	1990	Jill Trenary
1972	Janet Lynn	1991	Tonya Harding
1973	Janet Lynn	1992	Kristi Yamaguchi
1974	Dorothy Hamill	1993	Nancy Kerrigan
1975	Dorothy Hamill	1994	Vacant*
1976	Dorothy Hamill	1995	Nicole Bobek
1977	Linda Fratianne	1996	Michelle Kwan
1978	Linda Fratianne	1997	Tara Lipinski
1979	Linda Fratianne	1998	Michelle Kwan
1980	Linda Fratianne	1999	Michelle Kwan
1981	Elaine Zayak	2000	Michelle Kwan
1982	Rosalynn Sumners	2001	Michelle Kwan

* In June 1994, Tonya Harding was stripped of her title for her involvement in the Jan. 6, 1994, attack on Nancy Kerrigan. The USFSA Executive Committee voted to leave the title vacant for that year.

Men's Singles

1914	Norman M. Scott	1941	Eugene Turner
1915–7 No competitions		1942	Bobby Specht
1918	Nathaniel Niles	1943	Arthur Vaughn
1919	No competitions	1944–5 No competitions	
1920	Sherwin Badger	1946	Dick Button
1921	Sherwin Badger	1947	Dick Button
1922	Sherwin Badger	1948	Dick Button
1923	Sherwin Badger	1949	Dick Button
1924	Sherwin Badger	1950	Dick Button
1925	Nathaniel Niles	1951	Dick Button
1926	Chris Christenson	1952	Dick Button
1927	Nathaniel Niles	1953	Hayes A. Jenkins
1928	Roger Turner	1954	Hayes A. Jenkins
1929	Roger Turner	1955	Hayes A. Jenkins
1930	Roger Turner	1956	Hayes A. Jenkins
1931	Roger Turner	1957	David Jenkins
1932	Roger Turner	1958	David Jenkins
1933	Roger Turner	1959	David Jenkins
1934	Roger Turner	1960	David Jenkins
1935	Robin Lee	1961	Bradley Lord
1936	Robin Lee	1962	Monty Hoyt
1937	Robin Lee	1963	Thomas Litz
1938	Robin Lee	1964	Scott Allen
1939	Robin Lee	1965	Gary Visconti
1940	Eugene Turner	1966	Scott Allen

1967	Gary Visconti	1985	Brian Boitano
1968	Tim Wood	1986	Brian Boitano
1969	Tim Wood	1987	Brian Boitano
1970	Tim Wood	1988	Brian Boitano
1971	J. Misha Petkevich	1989	Christopher Bowman
1972	Kenneth Shelley	1990	Todd Eldredge
1973	Gordon McKellen	1991	Todd Eldredge
1974	Gordon McKellen	1992	Christopher Bowman
1975	Gordon McKellen	1993	Scott Davis
1976	Terry Kubicka	1994	Scott Davis
1977	Charles Tickner	1995	Todd Eldredge
1978	Charles Tickner	1996	Rudy Galindo
1979	Charles Tickner	1997	Todd Eldredge
1980	Charles Tickner	1998	Todd Eldredge
1981	Scott Hamilton	1999	Michael Weiss
1982	Scott Hamilton	2000	Michael Weiss
1983	Scott Hamilton	2001	Timothy Goebel
1984	Scott Hamilton		

Pair Skating

1914	Jean Chevalier Norman Scott	1929	Maribel Vinson Thornton Coolidge
1915–1917	No competitions	1930	Beatrix Loughran Sherwin Badger
1918	Theresa Weld Nathaniel Niles	1931	Beatrix Loughran Sherwin Badger
1919	No competitions	1932	Beatrix Loughran Sherwin Badger
1920	Theresa Weld Nathaniel Niles	1933	Maribel Vinson George Hill
1921	Theresa Blanchard Nathaniel Niles	1934	Grace Madden J. Lester Madden
1922	Theresa Blanchard Nathaniel Niles	1935	Maribel Vinson George Hill
1923	Theresa Blanchard Nathaniel Niles	1936	Maribel Vinson George Hill
1924	Theresa Blanchard Nathaniel Niles	1937	Maribel Vinson George Hill
1925	Theresa Blanchard Nathaniel Niles	1938	Joan Tozzer Bernard Fox
1926	Theresa Blanchard Nathaniel Niles	1939	Joan Tozzer Bernard Fox
1927	Theresa Blanchard Nathaniel Niles	1940	Joan Tozzer Bernard Fox
1928	Maribel Vinson Thornton Coolidge		

1941	Donna Atwood Eugene Turner	1954	Carole Ormaca Robin Greiner
1942	Doris Schubach Walter Noffke	1955	Carole Ormaca Robin Greiner
1943	Doris Schubach Walter Noffke	1956	Carole Ormaca Robin Greiner
1944	Doris Schubach Walter Noffke	1957	Nancy Rouillard Ronald Ludington
1945	Donna J. Pospisil Jean P. Brunet	1958	Nancy Ludington Ronald Ludington
1946	Donna J. Pospisil Jean P. Brunet	1959	Nancy Ludington Ronald Ludington
1947	Yvonne Sherman Robert Swenning	1960	Nancy Ludington Ronald Ludington
1948	Karol Kennedy Peter Kennedy	1961	Maribel Owen Dudley Richards
1949	Karol Kennedy Peter Kennedy	1962	Dorothyann Nelson Pieter Kollen
1950	Karol Kennedy Peter Kennedy	1963	Judianne Fotheringill Jerry Fotheringill
1951	Karol Kennedy Peter Kennedy	1964	Judianne Fotheringill Jerry Fotheringill
1952	Karol Kennedy Peter Kennedy	1965	Vivian Joseph Ronald Joseph
1953	Carole Ormaca Robin Greiner	1966	Cynthia Kauffman Ronald Kauffman

1967	Cynthia Kauffman Ronald Kauffman	1980	Tai Babilonia Randy Gardner
1968	Cynthia Kauffman Ronald Kauffman	1981	Caitlin Carruthers Peter Carruthers
1969	Cynthia Kauffman Ronald Kauffman	1982	Caitlin Carruthers Peter Carruthers
1970	Jojo Starbuck Kenneth Shelley	1983	Caitlin Carruthers Peter Carruthers
1971	Jojo Starbuck Kenneth Shelley	1984	Caitlin Carruthers Peter Carruthers
1972	Jojo Starbuck Kenneth Shelley	1985	Jill Watson Peter Oppegard
1973	Melissa Militano Mark Militano	1986	Gillian Wachsman Todd Waggoner
1974	Melissa Militano Johnny Johns	1987	Jill Watson Peter Oppegard
1975	Melissa Militano Johnny Johns	1988	Jill Watson Peter Oppegard
1976	Tai Babilonia Randy Gardner	1989	Kristi Yamaguchi Rudi Galindo
1977	Tai Babilonia Randy Gardner	1990	Kristi Yamaguchi Rudi Galindo
1978	Tai Babilonia Randy Gardner	1991	Natasha Kuchiki Todd Sand
1979	Tai Babilonia Randy Gardner	1992	Calla Urbanski Rocky Marval

1993	Calla Urbanski	1997	Kyoko Ina
	Rocky Marval		Jason Dungjen
1994	Jenni Meno	1998	Kyoko Ina
	Todd Sand		Jason Dungjen
1995	Jenni Meno	1999	Danielle Hartsell
	Todd Sand		Steve Hartsell
1996	Jenni Meno	2000	Kyoko Ina
	Todd Sand		John Zimmerman
		2001	Kyoko Ina
			John Zimmerman

Ice Dancing

1914   Theresa Weld & Nathaniel Niles

1915   No competition held

1916   No competition held

1917   No competition held

1918   No competition held

1919   No competition held

1920   Waltz: Theresa Weld & Nathaniel Niles
Ten Step: Gertrude Cheever Porter & Irving Brokaw

1921   Waltz: Theresa Weld Blanchard & Nathaniel Niles
Fourteen Step: Theresa Weld Blanchard & Nathaniel Niles

1922   Waltz: Beatrix Loughram & Edward Howland
Fourteen Step: Theresa Weld & Nathaniel Niles

1923   Waltz: Mrs. Henry Howe & Mr. Henry Howe
Fourteen Step: Sydney Goode & James Greene

1924   Watlz: Rosalie Dunn & Fredrik Gabel

Fourteeen Step: Sydney Goode & James Greene

1925   Waltz: Virginia Slattery & Ferrier Martin

Fourteen Step: Virginia Slattery & Ferrier Martin

1926   Waltz: Rosalie Dunn & Joseph Savage

Fourteen Step: Sydney Goode & James Greene

1927   Waltz: Rosalie Dunn & Joseph Savage

FourteenStep: Rosalie Dunn & Joseph Savage

1928   Waltz: Rosalie Dunn & Joseph Savage

Fourteen Step: Ada Baumann Kelly & George Braakman

1929   Waltz & Original Dance Combined:

Edith Secord & Joseph Savage

1930   Waltz: Edith Secord & Jopseph Savage

Original Dance: Clara Frothingham & George Hill

1931   Waltz: Edith Secord & Ferrier Martin

Original Dance: Theresa Weld Blanchard & Nathaniel Niles

1932   Waltz: Edith Secord & Joseph Savage

Original Dance: Clara Frothingham & George Hill

1933   Waltz: Ilse Twaroschk & Fred Fleischman

Original Dance: Suzanne Davis & Frederick Goodridge

1934   Waltz: Nettie Prantell & Roy Hunt

Original Dance: Suzanne Davis & Frederick Goodridge

1935   Waltz: Nettie Prantell & Roy Hunt

1936   Marjorie Parker & Joseph Savage

1937   Nettie Prantel & Harold Hartshorne

1938   Sandy MacDonald & Harold Hartshorne

1939   Sandy MacDonald & Harold Hartshorne

1940   Sandy MacDonald & Harold Hartshorne

1941   Sandy MacDonald & Harold Hartshorne

1942   Edith Whetstone & Alfred Richards

1943   Marcella May & James Lochead`

1944   Marcella May & James Lochead

1945   Kathe Williams & Robert Swenning

1946   Anne Davies & Carleton Hoffner

1947   Lois Waring & Walter Bainbridge

1948   Lois Waring & Walter Bainbridge

1949   Lois Waring & Walter Bainbridge

1950   Lois Waring & Michael McGean

1951   Carmel Bodel & Edward Bodel

1952   Lois Waring & Michael McGean

1953   Carol Ann Peters & Daniel Ryan

1954   Carmel Bodel & Edward Bodel

1955   Carmel Bodel & Edward Bodel

1956   Joan Zamboni & Roland Junso

1957   Sharon McKenzie & Bert Wright

1958   Andree Anderson & Donald Jacoby

1959   Andree Jacoby & Donald Jacoby

1960   Margie Ackles & Charles Phillips

1961   Dianne Sherbloom & Larry Pierce

1962   Yvonne Littlefield & Peter Betts

1963   Sally Schantz & Stanley Urban

1964   Darlene Streich & Charles Fetter

1965   Kristin Fortune & Dennis Sveum

1966   Kristin Fortune & Dennis Sveum

1967   Lorna Dyer & John Carrell

1968   Judy Schwomeyer & James Sladky

1969   Judy Schwomeyer & James Sladky

1970   Judy Schwomeyer & James Sladky

1971   Judy Schwomeyer & James Sladky

1972   Judy Schwomeyer & James Sladky

1973   Mary Campbell & Johnny Jones

1974   Colleen O'Connor & Jim Millns

1975   Colleen O'Connor & Jim Millns

1976   Colleen O'Connor & Jim Millns

1977   Judy Genovesi & Kent Weigle

1978   Stacey Smith & John Summers

1979   Stacey Smith & John Summers

1980   Stacey Smith & John Summers

1981   Judy Blumberg & Michael Seibert

1982   Judy Blumberg & Michael Seibert

1983   Judy Blumberg & Michael Seibert

1984   Judy Blumberg & Michael Seibert

1985   Judy Blumberg & Michael Seibert

1986   Renee Roca & Donald Adair

1987   Suzanne Semanick & Scott Gregory

1988   Suzanne Semanick & Scott Gregory

1989   Susan Wynne & Joseph Druar

1990   Susan Wynne & Joseph Druar

1991   Elizabeth Punsalan & Jerod Swallow

1992   April Sargent & Russ Witherby

1993   Renee Roca & Gorsha Sur

1994   Elizabeth Punsalan & Jerod Swallow

1995   Renee Roca & Gorsha Sur

1996   Elizabeth Punsalan & Jerod Swallow

1997   Elizabeth Punsalan & Jerod Swallow

1998   Elizabeth Punsalan & Jerod Swallow

1999   Naomi Lang & Peter Tchernyshev

2000   Naomi Lang & Peter Tchernyshev

2001   Naomi Lang & Peter Tchernyshev

2

Current American Skaters

WOMEN

Sarah Hughes

Sarah was born to a skating family in Great Neck, New York. Her two older brothers skated, as did her sister. Her father played hockey at Cornell University. So it was natural that she began skating at the age of three!

After capturing several novice competitions, Sarah made her breakthrough in 1998 when she won the U.S. Junior Championship. Since then, she has been a fierce competitor, finishing third in the 2001 World Championships and fifth in 2000. She finished second to Michelle Kwan in the 2001 U.S. Championships and came in third in 2000. She also finished first in both the 1999 Vienna Cup and the USA vs. World head-to-head competitions.

Like Tenley Albright, Sarah wants to study to become a doctor.

Doug Pensinger/ALLSPORT
Sara Hughes at the Chevrolet Skating Spectacular in 2001

Jennifer Kirk

It is natural that landing triple jumps is the favorite part of figure skating for Jennifer, who started skating at age nine after competing in gymnastics. A Massachusetts native, Jennifer was selected for four years to perform in the cast of the Boston Ballet *Nutcracker*. In addition to ballet and gymnastics, her other interests include piano, writing, art, and reading.

Jennifer finished first in the 2000 World Junior Championships. Her goal is to become a professional skater and top author.

Brian Bahr/ALLSPORT

Jennifer Kirk of the USA performs during the Women's short program of the 2001 Four Continents Championships.

Michelle Kwan

Michelle, who finished second in the 1998 Winter Olympic Games, has compiled a record unequaled in U.S. women's figure skating since Peggy Fleming. She has won four World Championships (1996, 1998, 2000, 2001), five U.S. Championships (1996, 1998, 1999, 2000, 2001), and one World Junior Championship (1994).

Michelle began skating at the age of five and won her first competition at age seven. She always wears a Chinese good luck charm around her neck that was given to her by her grandmother. She is a four-time recipient of *Skating* magazine's Readers Choice Award for figure skater of the year. In May 2000, she was named one of the "50 Most Beautiful People in the World" by *People* magazine.

A 5'2" dynamo, Michelle attends UCLA, trains at two locations in Southern California, has published an autobiography, *Michelle Kwan: Heart of a Champion*, and has even helped develop an interactive electronic video game for figure skating.

She is the first woman in figure skating history to reclaim the world title twice and has the most perfect (6.0) marks in major competition of any singles skater in the modern era.

Brian Bahr/ALLSPORT

Michelle Kwan skates the exhibition gala program
in the 2001 World Figure Skating Championships.

Angela Nikodinov

Angela began skating at the age of five. She placed fifth in the 2001 World Championships, having finished ninth in 2000 and 12th in 1999.

Other achievements include a first in the 2000 Four Continents Championships (she finished second in 2001) and a third at both the 1999 and 2001 U.S. Championships.

The athlete she admires most is speed skater Dan Jansen because of his determination and comeback to win Olympic gold.

Doug Pensinger/ALLSPORT

Angela Nikodinov skates her short program in the 2001 U.S. Figure
Skating Championships.

MEN

Todd Eldredge

One of the most decorated U.S. male figure skaters in history, Todd Eldredge has had his share of physical problems on his climb up the competition ladder. He was the U.S. men's champion in 1990 and 1991, then hurt his back. He lost a place on the U.S. Olympic Winter Games team in 1994 when a bad case of the flu prevented him from skating his best.

He regained his form and confidence and won the U.S. Championships again in 1995, 1997, and 1998. He won the World Championship in 1996 and finished second in 1997 and 1998.

Todd took off two years, 1999 and 2000, before returning to competition. He kept fit by playing golf, tennis, and basketball. In 2001 he finished second to Timothy Goebel in the U.S. Championships and third in the World Championships.

Brian Bahr/ALLSPORT
Todd Eldredge at the 2000 Skate America Competition

Timothy Goebel

Tim, who started skating at the age of four, is known as the "quad king." He is famous as the first American male to land a quadruple jump in competition. He is also the first skater ever to land a quadruple salchow and a quadruple salchow-triple combination in the World Championships. Moreover, he is the first skater to land three quadruple jumps in one performance in competition.

Tim placed second in the U. S Championships in 2000 and first in 2001. He placed fourth in the 2001 World Championships, up from 11th in 2000. He is an honor student who trains in El Segundo, California.

Brian Bahr/ALLSPORT

Timothy Goebel finishes in first place at
the 2000 Skate America Competition.

Matt Savoie

Matt began skating at the age of nine. Since 1993 he has consistently performed well in numerous competitive junior events. He finished third in the 2000 World Junior Championships and fourth in the U.S. Championships.

Matt enjoys reading, bike riding, and rollerblading and most admires Scott Hamilton and Michael Jordan. One day he hopes to pursue a career in the field of biology.

Brian Bahr/ALLSPORT

Matt Savoie of the USA performs during the
Men's Short Program of the 2001 Four Continents
Championships.

Michael Weiss

Michael started skating at the age of nine in his native Washington, D.C. He has worked hard and made significant progress each year. He won the U.S. Junior Championship in 1993, then moved from eighth in the 1994 U.S. Championships to sixth in 1995, fifth in 1996, second in 1997 and 1998, and first in 1999 and 2000.

He did much the same in the World Championships, going from first in the Junior World Championship in 1994 to third in the World Championship in 1999 and 2000. Michael earned a seventh-place finish in the 1998 Winter Olympic Games.

Michael has received the 2000 *Skating* magazine Readers Choice Award for skater of the year, the 2000 USFSA/USOC Male Figure Skater of the Year Award, and 1999 Father of the Year honors from the National Fatherhood Initiative. He is married to his choreographer, the former Lisa Thornton, and has two children.

Jamie McDonald/ALLSPORT

Michael Weiss skates his short program at
the 2000 U.S. Figure Skating Championships.

PAIRS

Kyoko Ina and John Zimmerman

Both Kyoko and John began skating at early ages—four and three, respectively. While both have skated with other partners, since they started skating together in 1998 they have won many medals.

After finishing second in the 1999 U.S. Championships, they won their first U.S. Championship title in 2000, and repeated with a first in 2001. They placed seventh in the 2000 and 2001 World Championships.

Kyoko's other interests include jet-skiing, horseback riding, tennis, and car racing, while John's other interests include rock climbing, rollerblading, mountain biking, and watching auto racing. Kyoko aspires to be a television commentator, and John is pursuing a degree in business.

Doug PensingerALLSPORT

Kyoko Ina and John Zimmerman at the
2001 World Figure Skating Championships

ICE DANCING

Tanith Belbin and Benjamin Agosto

Skating together since 1998, this ice dance duo placed first in the 2000 U.S. Junior Championships and third in the 2000 World Junior Championships. In addition to ice dancing, Tanith enjoys dancing and singing, and Benjamin likes to play the guitar and keyboard.

Brian Bahr/ALLSPORT

Tanith Belbin and Benjamin Agosto of the USA perform during
the original dance portion of the ice dancing competition at the
2001 World Figure Skating Championships.

Naomi Lang and Peter Tchernyshev

Naomi and Peter have been ice dancing together in competition since 1997. They have won three U.S. Championships, in 1999, 2000, and 2001. In the World Championships, they finished tenth in 1999, eighth in 2000, and ninth in 2001.

Naomi, who was born in Arcata, California, began skating when she was eight years old after seeing the Ice Capades. She has also danced as a member of the Grand Rapids, Michigan, Ballet Company.

Peter was born in St. Petersburg, Russia, and is the grandson of a four-time Russian singles figure skating champion (1936-1939).

Naomi and Peter train in Hackensack, New Jersey.

Doug Pensinger/ALLSPORT

Naomi Lang and Peter Tchernyshev at the
2001 Chevrolet Skating Spectacular

3

The First Time at the Ice Rink

The best way to get started in figure skating is simply to rent a pair of skates and try the ice. If you're a first-timer, take a friend or family member who knows how to skate to show you how to get started with the basic push-glide strokes. Some rinks offer first-time skaters a free lesson along with their skate rental.

Each skate consists of a boot and a blade. Blades are approximately 1/8-inch wide. The groove running the length of the blade is called a "hollow." The hollow gives each blade two edges, an inside edge and an outside edge. These edges are what skaters use to grip the ice when skating in curves and circles. The teeth, or toe picks, are at the front of the blade. When you are an advanced skater, you'll use them to start your jumps and spins.

Basic Position—The First Basic Skill

Before going on the ice for the first time, beginning ice skaters need to learn the *basic position*. Try this off the ice, with your skate guards on.

- Spread your legs as far apart as your shoulders, with your feet parallel and toes straight ahead. This is your normal stand-up position, except now you're wearing ice skates, not street shoes.
- Bend slightly, so your knees push forward over the toe of your skates and your hips move slightly backward (as though you were starting to sit down on a chair).
- Your weight should be over your arches on the balls of your feet, not leaning back or forward.
- Your hips and shoulders should be squared, not off to one side or hunched.
- Keep your head in a natural, comfortable position, looking ahead, not down.
- Keep your arms at your sides, slightly bent at the elbows, so your hands are slightly in front of you and about as high as your hips. Do not hold your arms straight out.

Natural Balance—The Second Basic Skill

To find your *natural balance,* remove your skate guards and get on the ice while holding on to the railing or any other support.

- While holding on to a support with one hand, hold the other arm out from your side.
- Slide your feet back and forth in short strides. This will give you a "feel" for the ice.
- Weight should be over the middle of your skate blades where your foot arches. Be sure your skates do not tilt out or lean in on the edges.
- While still holding on, lift one foot 2–3 inches off the ice. Then put your foot down and raise the other foot. Continue to shift your weight from foot to foot a few times.
- Practice this again without holding on, holding your arms away from your body as you did for the basic position.
- Shift your weight back and forth from one foot to the other and try taking a few small steps.
- Try some longer steps.

- Use your arms to help you keep your balance. Be sure to stay close to the railing in case you need support.
- Stand still on the ice.
- Do several knee bends with and without support.

Learning the basic position and finding your natural balance will take practice. You'll need to master these two basic skills before you can go on to actual skating.

Falling

Everyone falls on the ice—even the champions. To avoid getting hurt and endangering others, you will need to learn how to fall and get up properly.

Falling properly is a skill you can practice while you're off the ice. This will help you understand what happens when you fall, so that when it happens on the ice you'll be ready to get right back up and start skating again.

When you fall, try to sit down easily on your bottom or thighs. Relax. Sonja Henie's brother taught her to think of falling as though her body were a flexible, untied rope, and not a rigid piece of wood or metal. Learning to stay "loose" will help you avoid breaking bones.

When you fall, remember to keep your fingers away from your blades. Try to protect your head as much as possible. After you fall, get up properly and quickly. Other skaters will have a much harder time seeing you when you are down on the ice.

One easy way to get up quickly after you fall is first to support yourself on your hands and knees. Then bring one foot even with the opposite knee and put your skate blade flat on the ice. Repeat this for the other foot, put your arms out in front, and stand up slowly.

Pushing Off and Gliding

Other basic skills are pushing off and gliding. Both are required for any kind of skating. To push off and start your glide:

- Stand straight, with your skates hip-width apart and toes even.
- Take the basic position, with your knees bent slightly.
- Shift your body's weight onto your left foot. Put the back of your right foot in front of your left instep to form a "T." Tilt your left ankle over and feel the inside edge of your left skate grip the ice.
- Bend both knees and push from that left inside edge toward your right foot. Your weight should shift to the right skate, and you will feel the push from the left foot and start to glide.
- Once the weight is on your right foot, gently lift your left foot off the ice until you are gliding on only your right skate. You should be gliding on the middle to back of the blade.

To keep on gliding:

- Bring your left leg and skate back alongside your right leg and skate. You will be gliding on both feet in the basic position.
- Repeat all of the above, only this time push off with your right foot.
- Alternate feet. First push off with the left foot, then with the right.
- Start with short glides. Lengthen your strokes as you become more confident in shifting from one skate to the other and balancing.
- Hold one leg off the ice longer. This creates longer glides and shortens the time when gliding with your skates together.

All these skills, when properly practiced, make figure skating and plain stroking beautiful to watch and enjoyable to do.

Stopping

Beginners often stop by skating toward the edge of the rink and grabbing the barrier or railing with both hands. The best way to stop is the T-stop, the stop used in figure skating.

- Glide with your feet parallel, using the same position you learned to use between gliding strokes.
- Lift your right foot and put it behind your left foot, with your right instep against the heel of your left foot. Your feet will be in a "T."
- Turn your right shoulder, arm, and hip backward; your left shoulder, arm, and hip forward. Your body—but not your head—will be sideways.

Courtesy on the Ice

Skating is one of the safer sports, but it can become unsafe if skaters forget to follow the rules and don't use common sense. Skating is also an individual sport, with practice sessions fairly unstructured. Some basic rules must be observed for safety and to ensure that all skaters can make good use of their ice time. Each rink or club will have its own set of rules, which are usually posted. Make sure you know the rules and always follow them. Here are some rules that are common to most clubs and rinks:

- First is courtesy. Respect the rights of other skaters. Be aware of who is around you. Try hard to avoid collisions.
- Most rinks establish an order of priority. The skater "doing a program" (whose music is playing) has the right of way at all times. Second in priority are skaters who are in lessons. Always yield to these skaters.
- On days when the ice rink is filled with skaters—or even when the rink is relatively empty—a common practice for public sessions is to skate in a counterclockwise direction. The middle of the rink may be for figure skating only. Everyone else skates near the outer edge.

- Don't stop on the ice to chat with a friend, to retie your boots, or for any other reason. Off the ice is the safe place to take a break. Stopping can lead to a chain-reaction collision of skaters.
- Have fun while skating, certainly, but don't clown around or be aggressive toward other skaters. And don't attempt dangerous moves.
- When you fall, get back up and start skating right away. This rule doesn't apply if a skater is seriously hurt, of course (see Chapter 11, "Basic Safety and First Aid").
- Never take food or beverages on the ice.
- Before skating backward, look behind you to make sure the way is clear. Even in the middle of the ice, a skater must check to see that there is plenty of room to practice jumps, spins, and other moves.

Remember, skate blades are sharp and can cause serious wounds to even accomplished skaters, as sisters Carol and Nancy Heiss learned just before the 1954 World Championships. The two were skating backward toward each other and collided. The muscles of Carol's left leg were cut by the sharp edge of Nancy's skate, and she damaged her Achilles tendon as well. It took nearly a year of rehabilitation and practice before Carol Heiss was back on the ice. She eventually won an Olympic gold medal in 1960.

4

Figure Skating Skills

Figure skating is a moving sport. Participants are always moving forward or backward, jumping, or spinning. The trick is to do all that gliding, jumping, and spinning in a graceful, choreographed order. That's where the skill comes in.

We tend to think of the "big stuff"—the jumps and spins—as the most important parts of skating because they are the most exciting. But successful figure skaters know that *all* of the elements are important.

Connecting Elements

Connecting elements are all the movements that go in between the jumps and spins. The variety of connecting elements is limited only by the skater's imagination and skill.

In Chapter 1 we discussed how the term "figure skating" came from requiring skaters to trace figures on the ice over and over. Not until much later were jumps and spins even allowed in competition.

Doug Pensinger /ALLSPORT

Todd Eldredge demonstrates a connecting move

Moves in the field (MIF) requirements now form the basis for all edges and turns in skating. (For more on MIF, see Chapter 7, "Proficiency Tests for Figure Skaters.")

Simple Turns

Some elements such as one-foot turns are part of MIF and are also used extensively in free skating routines. Here are some simple one-foot turns you'll see every skater use.

- **Three turn:** This is a one-foot turn that is in the shape of the number 3. With this turn you stay in the same circle but change direction and edge. For instance, a three turn started on a left forward outside edge finishes on a left back inside edge.
- **Rocker turn:** The rocker changes circle and direction but maintains the same edge. For example, a rocker entered on the right forward outside edge will finish on the right back outside edge.

Two-Foot Turns

Two-foot turns involve both feet. While they may sound twice as difficult as a one-foot turn, they're not. The two best known two-foot turns are the Mohawk and the Choctaw. No one seems to be able to explain why these turns are named after Native American tribes.

- **Mohawk:** The skater steps forward by going backward to forward, changing feet but keeping the same edge. Alternatively, the skater steps back by going forward to backward, changing feet but keeping the same edge. For example, the skater will be going forward on the inside edge of the right skate, then step over onto the inside edge of the left skate going backward. Mohawk turns are used before jumps or to change direction quickly.
- **Choctaw:** This turn can be a bit tricky. It requires that skaters change feet, change direction, and change edge. If a skater is going forward on the right outside edge, he or she must step over to the left inside edge and change to a backward direction. This movement is most frequently performed in footwork sequences. It is dramatic and unusual, and usually remembered by the judges.

Graceful Movements

An important part of any figure skating program is moving gracefully, with controlled, flowing movements that demonstrate balance and mastery of the basic skating skills. What follows is a brief description of two movements which, when done well, look particularly graceful.

- **Spirals:** The spiral is one of the most beautiful and graceful moves. To perform a spiral, a skater glides forward or backward in a circle on one foot, while raising the nonskating leg backward in the air. The object is to keep the nonskating leg up as high as the hip or higher, with the head looking up.

- **Spread-eagle**: For this movement, a skater will glide in a "spread-eagle" position with legs spread apart, toes out, and heels in a heel-to-heel alignment. The skater's chest will be facing perpendicular to the direction of the skates. The skater leans back to skate on the outside edges of the skates, or leans slightly forward to skate on the inside edges.

Spins

Spins are an important part of any free skating program. A good spin meets four criteria—speed, aesthetic line, balance, and centering (the degree to which the skater stays in one place on the ice while spinning). While there are many different kinds of spins, there are only three spin positions: upright spins, sit spins, and camel spins. Like jumps, spins can be performed individually or in combination with another spin position.

Brian Bahr/ALLSPORT

Michelle Kwan does a sit spin at the
U.S. Figure Skating Championships in 1999.

- **Upright spins:** For an upright spin, the skater will remain in the upright skating position. There are one-foot spins (performed on either foot) and two-foot spins in this position.
- **Sit spins:** For a sit spin, a skater is not really sitting; instead, the skater squats on one leg, with the nonskating (free) leg extended straight out in front. The lower a skater can squat, the better the spin will be marked. Like the upright spin, the sit can be performed on either foot.
- **Camel spins:** To do a camel spin, a skater puts his or her body into a "T" shape, with one leg skating and the nonskating (free) leg held straight out behind. Again, this spin can be performed with either foot.

Good spins are fast and centered. Keys to a high mark include an attractive blending of arms, hands, legs, and overall body movement; the number of revolutions (more is better); and the ability to stay in one place and not travel across the ice during the spin.

Jumps

Did you turn to this page first? A lot of people do, because everybody loves the jumps. But did you know there are many different kinds and combinations of jumps? And did you know that the position of the feet on takeoff is what determines how successful the jump will be? Skaters always land on one skate after a jump, usually the right skate. And most jumps are done so fast that it is difficult to tell one from another. Here are some things to look for when watching or learning jumps.

Toe Jumps

Skaters who start with a quick assist from the toe picks of their skate on the nonskating foot are doing a toe-assisted jump, or a toe jump. Toe jumps are perfectly legal. They include standards like the toe loop and lutz jumps.

Edge Jumps

Jumps that start with no assistance from a toe pick are called edge jumps. Edge jumps are harder to do, and receive higher scores when successful. Examples of edge jumps are axels, salchows, and loops.

Direction at Takeoff

The takeoff position for most jumps is while the skater is going backward. The only common jumps for which this is not true are the waltz jump and the axel, which makes them easy to spot and anticipate.

Brian Bahr/ALLSPORT

Timothy Goebel does a small jump at the
World Figure Skating Championships in 2001.

Direction of Rotation

Most jumps are naturally rotating; the direction of the rotation in the air is the same direction as the curve that the skater was skating before the jump. A counter-rotated jump, such as the lutz, is more difficult because the direction of the jump rotation is the opposite of that in which the skater's body was moving on the ice.

Brian Bahr/ALLSPORT   Matthew Stockman/ALLSPORT
Timothy Goebel (left) and Michael Tylleson (right) demonstrate jumps.

Small Jumps

Skaters use a huge variety of "small" jumps either individually or as connecting elements in free skating programs. A visit to a good skating Web site or a trip to the library to check out a book on jumps will give you detailed descriptions. Be sure to look up some of the most popular small jumps, such as the split jump, the Russian split, the stag, the bunny hop, the falling leaf, and the half flip.

Some Final Words About Jumps

There are many varieties of advanced jumps, such as the axel, loop, salchow, and lutz. Many are covered in the Glossary (see Chapter 13). All of the jumps described can be done as individual jumps, doubles, or triples, or in combinations with other jumps.

Skaters who successfully complete multiple-revolution jumps (doubles and triples) do them the same way they would do a single-revolution jump, except that the revolutions are tighter and the spins faster. It is easy to see the difference between singles and doubles. To see the difference between doubles and triples you will have to watch closely to observe the tighter rotational position.

Marks are generally based on the difficulty of the jump. In ascending order of difficulty, the jumps are the salchow, toe loop, loop, flip, lutz, and axel. Each added revolution increases the difficulty of the jump. Judges evaluate the jumps for speed flowing into and out of the jump, the height of the jump (higher is better), a clean takeoff, and a clean and a solid landing, all executed with overall control throughout the jump.

Many American skaters were the first to complete some of the most difficult jumps in official competition:

- Dick Button completed a double axel in the 1948 Olympic Games.
- Carol Heiss was the first woman to complete a double axel, in 1953.
- Dick Button completed the first triple loop (the first-ever triple jump) in the 1952 Olympics.
- Ronald Robertson completed a triple salchow in the 1955 World Championships.
- Thomas Litz completed a triple toe loop in the 1964 World Championships.
- Timothy Goebel completed the first quadruple salchow and also the first quadruple salchow-triple jump combination, at the 1999 World Championships.
- In the 1997 U.S. Nationals, Tara Lipinski was the first woman to complete a triple/triple loop.

5

United States Figure Skating Association (USFSA)

While Jackson Haines gave America its first taste of the International Style in figure skating, it required the efforts in the late 1800s of three other figure skating pioneers—Louis Rubenstein, George H. Browne, and Irving Brokaw—before the International Style secured its place in the American figure skating community. All three men saw the need for a national governing body to organize the sport and to standardize tests and competitions using consistent rules.

History of the USFSA

In the late 1800s, Rubenstein, a Canadian, was one of the first individuals to recognize the benefits of the International Style and the need for organization in the sport. He helped to organize the Amateur Skating Association of Canada, which was established in 1887; the group later changed its name to the

Canadian Figure Skating Association and has been known since 2000 as Skate Canada. Rubenstein also helped found the National Amateur Skating Association of the United States and the International Skating Union of America. Both of these organizations were forerunners of the United States Figure Skating Association (USFSA).

While Rubenstein helped to establish uniform competition and tests, George H. Browne and Irving Brokaw of Cambridge, Massachusetts, great supporters of the International Style of skating, organized the first International Figure Skating Championships. Held in the United States in 1914 under the guidance of the International Skating Union of America (ISU of A)—the governing body for both speed and figure skating in the early 1900s—the competition was created to promote the International Style and to streamline figure skating in the United States.

Building on the work of the ISU of A, as well as on Browne's efforts in creating uniform standards, the USFSA was formed in 1921 to govern the sport and promote its growth in the United States.

Before the USFSA was founded, figure skating competitions in the United States were conducted under rules and regulations that varied from club to club and competition to competition. Skaters decided if they were qualified and were free to enter any competitions.

Today, the USFSA has more than 585 member clubs, sanctions over 1,250 events for its nearly 150,000 members, and promotes the sport with publications, clinics, financial assistance, and extraordinary energy. Through its television productions, World Wide Web site (http://www.usfsa.org/), and *Skating* magazine, the USFSA has helped figure skating become one of the most popular Olympic sports. In recent years, more than 1,000 figure skaters have competed in the U.S. Championships.

By performing successfully at regional, sectional, and national championships, USFSA member skaters may qualify to enter the Winter Olympic Games and/or the World Championships.

The USFSA administers compulsory and free skating tests at nine skill levels: pre-preliminary, preliminary, pre-juvenile, juvenile, intermediate, novice, junior, senior, and adult. Skaters must pass the tests in one or more of these figure skating disciplines: singles (women's or men's), pairs, ice dancing, and synchronized team skating. (See Chapter 8, "Competitive Figure Skating.")

USFSA Programs

The USFSA has developed a variety of programs for figure skaters, their parents, coaches, and the general public. These include programs for financial assistance, training, academic scholarships, and grassroots participation.

Here is a brief look at some of the offerings by the Athlete Development Committee. A visit to the Web site will explain each in detail.

U.S. Team Envelope System

This USFSA program's function is to identify champion-quality figure skaters in the United States. These skaters are offered financial assistance and training, and are placed in one of five envelopes: Team A, Team B, Team C, Reserve Team, and Development Team D. Each team envelope placement is determined by a skater's ranking at the previous year's World Championships, World Junior Championships, U.S. Championships, and Junior Olympics.

USFSA/Chevrolet Team 2006

This is one of the programs developed by the USFSA Athlete Development Committee to educate skaters, coaches, and parents. Participants spend two days getting acquainted, building team spirit, and using this opportunity to promote figure skaters and figure skating. The program includes emphasis on judging, media training, off-ice training concepts, and psychological development. Key presenters for the sessions are national referees, judges, and officials.

Leading Ph.D.'s in sports psychology as well as master athletic trainers provide the leadership for the psychology and conditioning classes.

USFSA Sports Science Camps

These camps, held since 1978, give top-level figure skaters an opportunity to meet with physicians, nutrition experts, coaches, sports psychologists, fitness experts, and other professionals who help skaters to improve their overall performance and learn to maintain injury-free good health.

Chevrolet/USFSA Skate with U.S. Basic Skills

This is a grassroots, basic skills program currently sponsored by Chevrolet and the USFSA. Its goal since 1985 has been to promote ice skating among skaters at all levels, from tiny tots to senior citizens. More than 350,000 people have joined and participated in at least one of the nine skill levels: Snowplow Sam, Basic Skills, Freestyle, Power Freestyle, Figures, Dance, Team, Hockey, and Power Hockey.

Memorial Fund

The Memorial Fund was established in memory of the members of the U.S. World Figure Skating Team who died in an airplane crash in 1961. The fund provides qualified USFSA skaters in need of financial aid with monetary assistance. Skating and academic scholarships are awarded to athletes who have demonstrated excellent competitive results and/or academic achievements and who have future potential in national and international competitions.

Museum and Hall of Fame

In addition to the above programs, the USFSA sponsors the World Figure Skating Museum. Here, figure skating history is preserved at a one-of-a-kind facility located at USFSA headquarters in Colorado Springs, Colorado. Also at this location is the U.S. Figure Skating Hall of Fame, which honors amateur and professional U.S. skaters, coaches, and officials.

For more information on the USFSA, contact the organization at the following address:

United States Figure Skating Association
20 First Street
Colorado Springs, CO 80906
phone: (719) 635–5200
fax: (719) 635–9548
Internet: http://www.usfsa.org/
e-mail: usfsa@usfsa.org

6

Training, Equipment, and Clothing

A major benefit of figure skating is that the fitness you develop while learning and training will carry over to any other sports or recreational activities you enjoy, such as soccer, gymnastics, swimming, or biking.

If you decide to get serious about skating, you will want to consider taking group or private lessons and joining a figure skating club affiliated with the USFSA. Many rinks have qualified instructors for skaters at all levels, from preschool to adult. Group lessons are a great way to start. They teach teamwork, sportsmanship, commitment, and dependability.

There are no age restrictions or strict physical requirements for figure skaters. Some famous skaters —for example, Dick Button—didn't begin skating seriously until they were almost in their teens. Button was 12 years old when he started regular lessons, but just six years later he was an Olympic gold medal winner.

Tenley Albright started skating when she was nine, but contracted polio when she was 11 and had to stop skating. As soon as she was able, she began skating and training again to strengthen her back muscles and regain her confidence. Six years later, in 1952, Albright won the first of five consecutive U.S. Women's Figure Skating Championships.

Kristi Yamaguchi, the 1992 Winter Olympic Games gold medal winner in women's singles, was born with club (deformed) feet. As a small child she had to wear casts to correct the condition. She took ballet lessons when she was four, and began skating at five. By her 21st birthday, she had won the World Championships two years in a row, been U.S. champion, and finished with a gold medal at the Albertville Olympics.

Skating Rinks, Clubs, and Coaches

To locate a skating rink, a figure skating club, or a coach, you can call your local department of parks and recreation, look under "skating" in a business telephone directory, use the Internet, or call the USFSA or the Professional Skaters Association (PSA).

Vincent Laforet/ALLSPORT

A Zamboni® machine sets down a layer of new ice.

Jed Jacobson/ALLSPORT

Michelle Kwan and her coach Frank Carroll at the 1996
World Figure Skating Championships

Before making a selection, you need to consider how serious
you are about skating. A serious commitment will mean practices
of 45 to 60 minutes, two to three times per week. Beyond the
time commitment, you'll need transportation, some costly
equipment, and the support of family and friends. It's a good
idea to talk with a coach and get some guidance before dedicating
yourself to skating in competition.

Selecting a coach is a big decision. Your relationship with skating instructors or coaches usually begins when you take your first group lesson. Several instructors generally teach group lessons. During this time you will be able to meet and work with several different instructors. You should pay attention to their different coaching styles and techniques, their personalities, and their compatibility with your skating interests. Once you are ready to advance from group lessons, you will want to select a coach. Talk to other skaters and their parents to find out what the instructors are like as coaches. Interview the coaches you are interested in and watch them working with their other students.

Believe it or not, one of the essential elements of competitive skating is to rent or sign up for a section of the ice rink where you can practice. That's because practicing requires a circular space with freshly cleaned ice. Many rinks have a Zamboni® machine that resurfaces the ice periodically to keep it clean.

Buying and Caring for Equipment

Boots and blades for a beginner's skates can be purchased for about $40, with the cost rising to $500 or more as the skater moves up the competitive ladder.

Blades

When buying skates, be sure to buy all-tempered steel blades. Figure skating blades manufactured from very hard all-tempered steel will stay sharp and not need to be re-sharpened as often as blades made from steel that is only partly tempered.

Attaching blades to boots is not a do-it-yourself project, since each blade must be carefully screwed on and set properly in the boot's sole. The same can be said for sharpening blades. Professionals have the training and equipment for both sharpening and correctly attaching blades, so it's best to let them help you (especially when you are getting started).

Boots

IOC/ALLSPORT

A modern figure skate

When buying boots, the number-one consideration for figure skaters at any level is that the boot fit well. Skates should be worn with tights or thin socks, not thick or bulky socks. If you buy skates that are too large, and pad them with heavy socks, you will find them uncomfortable to wear and nearly impossible to skate in. This will quickly take the fun out of skating.

The fit should be comfortable. The boot should be snug around the ankle and heel, with some "wiggle" room for movement of the toes so there is no pinching. The heel should fit snugly to avoid rubbing that could cause blisters. The boot should also have a sturdy, well-positioned arch support. The very best (and most expensive) skates are custom made for the individual skater. However, good ready-made skates for beginners can be found at rink pro shops and sporting goods stores.

Lacing Your Skates

Lacing skates is important. Learning how to lace your skates is easy.

- Loosen the laces, pull the tongue forward, and insert your foot into the boot. Center the boot tongue and pull it up.
- Tighten the laces through the eyelets so that they are snug but not tight. Leave wiggle room. To ensure proper support for the ankles, the tightest point of lacing should be at the instep.
- Crisscross the laces snugly around each hook.

- When you reach the top hook, tie a secure bow. If the ends are too long, tuck them into your boot. Do not let them drag on the ice.
- A good fit will allow enough space for you to insert a finger in the back of each boot. Once you have finished lacing your boots, walk around in the skates off the ice. Your foot and ankle should feel secure and comfortable in the boot.

Steve Powell/ALLSPORT

Competitors take good care of their figure skates.

Caring for Figure Skates

You spend a lot of money on your skates, so you need to take care of them properly. To keep your skates and blades in tip-top condition, follow these suggestions.

Blades

- Skate blades are thin, sharp, and fragile. They should be worn with hard skate guards when you are off the ice for a break or are finished skating. When you get off the ice, dry off your blades before you put on the guards. Blade guards are available in colorful rubber or plastic, in sizes to fit most blades. They can be purchased at pro shops or sport stores.

- Blades are made to slide on ice, not walk on floors. When you have to walk on floors, put hard guards on your blades.
- Always dry off your blades when you get off the ice. Make sure you also dry the hollow and the mounting surfaces, including the screws.
- To protect against rust, terry cloth blade covers, or soakers, are used when your skates are stored after practice or competition. Never store your blades in hard guards because they hold moisture and cause rusting.
- Keep your blades sharp. A sharp blade grabs the ice better than a dull blade. Sharpen your blades if they start to slide when you land or if they begin to skid sideways when pushing or doing crossovers. Have an expert sharpen your skate blades. NEVER have them sharpened by an automatic blade-sharpening machine.
- Check regularly for missing or loose blade screws.

Boots

- Coat the heels and soles of your skate boots with a leather enamel, available at pro shops.
- Water can damage the leather of your boots. Keep your boots polished at all times, or use a leather preserver to keep your boots soft, flexible, and looking good. Leather preservers are usually available at pro shops.
- Let the inside of your boot air dry. Moisture gets trapped inside because your feet sweat when you skate. Loosen laces, pull out the tongue, and let the insides of your skates dry.
- To store your skates: undo the laces, wrap the boots in heavy paper, and store in a cool, dry place where the air can circulate.
- Carry your skates in a boot bag. Don't dangle them or sling them over your shoulders

Clothes

It's important to stay warm—but not too warm—when skating. Avoid going outside to skate when the weather is too cold, as you run the risk of serious illness. Wear comfortable clothes, in layers you can easily remove. Stay away from long dresses or slacks that are wide and loose. These can cause falls and other accidents.

All you need for practices are tights in a blend of cotton, nylon, and spandex, and a long-sleeved top. You may want to add leg warmers, a sweater, and gloves or mittens if the weather is cold. If it's *really* cold, you can add a warmup suit and wool boot covers.

Leave jewelry in a safe place. Any object that drops on the ice is a hazard to all skaters. Long hair should be tied back during practices and competitions.

Competitions are showcases for skating ability, not costumes. Female figure skaters wear tights and a leotard with a skirt that covers the hips and bottom. If skating in competition, you can choose an outfit that reflects the mood of the music. No props are allowed: items such as feathers or jewelry can fall on the ice and pose a danger to skaters.

In competition, men wear a one- or two-piece outfit or suit that must have sleeves. Pair skaters often wear costumes that complement each other in style and color. No skater is allowed to use props or wear inappropriate clothing.

Skaters who want to compete in sanctioned events must pass certain tests of skating proficiency administered by the USFSA.

7

Proficiency Tests for Figure Skaters

General Testing Procedures

When you and your coach decide that you are ready for your first test, or to move to the next level, you must apply at a USFSA club for the appropriate test, and pay a fee. Your test time will be posted a few days before the actual test. There may be other skaters tested on the same date and at the same place.

Three judges selected by the USFSA club usually administer tests. To ensure fairness, judges cannot be related to the skater or coach. Depending on your test level, the judges will be near you on the ice or seated close to the rink.

The Judge-in-Charge is the only judge who will talk to you and give you instructions. For tests with more than one part, you will skate the first part, then wait on the ice until you are told to skate the second part. Don't leave the ice until the Judge-in-Charge excuses you, for you may be asked to reskate a part of your test.

You'll get the results of your test that same day, so there will be no worrying or watching the mailbox for results. The judges will give you a "pass" or "retry" grade and write comments on your test sheets. In order for you to be successful, two of the three judges must give you a grade of "pass." If you receive a grade of "retry," you can go back to work with your coach and prepare to take the test again after 28 days have passed.

Simon Bruty/ALLSPORT

The judges' table at the 1994 Winter Olympics

Judges

Judges go through a process of extensive trial judging and promotions by the test chair. As a result, they are well qualified to evaluate your test. They understand how nervous you are, and how much you want to succeed. Like your parents, teachers, and coaches, they want to you to perform to the established standards and pass the tests. Be aware, however, that no judge will award passing marks to any skater who is not prepared for the test.

If there are four judges at your test, chances are that the fourth is learning how to be a figure skating judge. This will require extra time while the three regular judges explain some of the points of judging to the fourth. Only the three assigned judges will award your marks.

At higher-level competitions, the judges often watch practice sessions in order to become familiar with the skaters' programs and skills. There are no instant replays during the actual competition, and watching practices provides the judges an advance look at how difficult a program might be and gives them a preview of what to look for on the ice.

Proficiency Test Requirements

Proficiency is what counts in testing. There are no age requirements for the skill levels, although some age restrictions apply for competitions. The tests cover six skill levels or categories: figures, moves in the field (MIF), free skating, pair skating, dance, and synchronized. For complete details, consult the *2001 Official USFSA Rule Book*.

Figures

Figures, once the foundation of compulsories for all competitive skating, were eliminated from international competition in the 1991–1992 season and were last competed at the U.S. Championships in 1999. The figures themselves are edges and turns, which are the basis of freestyle skating movement. Figures tests start with a beginner's Preliminary Test and progress through the highest and most difficult Eighth Test.

Moves in the Field (MIF)

These are technical disciplines a skater uses to master the basic skills. All the components of figures are incorporated into patterns that utilize the entire ice surface. Edge quality, power (speed and flow), quickness (foot speed) and extension, and general carriage are emphasized. There are eight MIF tests. Each MIF level contains essential building blocks of skills that must be mastered before a skater is ready to progress to the next level.

Pre-Preliminary Tests

Free skating—Demonstrate command of the following elements: waltz jump; salchow; toe loop; half flip (landing on whichever foot); half lutz (landing on whichever foot); and a one-foot spin.

MIF—Perform the following: perimeter stroking; basic consecutive edges (forward inside and outside, backward inside and outside); and a waltz eight.

Preliminary Tests

Free skating—Demonstrate command of the waltz jump; salchow; loop; flip; one jump combination; a one-foot upright spin; a one-foot back spin; and a sit spin.

MIF—Perform forward and backward crossovers; consecutive outside and inside spirals; forward three turns; alternating forward three turns; and alternating backward crossovers to backward outside edges.

Pair skating—Perform a single jump; a pair spin with no change of foot or position; a solo spin; one lift; stroking forward, backward, clockwise, and counterclockwise; and footwork and connecting moves.

Dance—Perform the Dutch waltz, canasta tango, and rhythm blues.

Free dance—Ice dancers must perform the following: (a) three positions from Group I—kilian, fox-trot (open), waltz (closed), hand in hand, cross-arm (backwards); (b) one lift from group II—spiral lift, straight arm lift, fox-trot lift, any other lift or variation; (c) one element from Group III—lay over, pull through legs, side pull, front drop, side-by-side lunge, assisted shoot-the-duck, any assisted dance jump, any original move; and (d) footwork with one- and two-foot turns.

Pre-Juvenile Tests

Free skating—Demonstrate command over the following elements: loop; flip; lutz; one jump combo; a camel spin; a combo camel to sit spin; front scratch spin to back scratch spin; and connecting moves and steps.

MIF—Perform forward perimeter power crossover stroking; backward perimeter power crossover stroking; three turns; forward and backward power change of edge pulls; and a five-step Mohawk sequence. (*Note: Power stroking is stroking in a corkscrew pattern of gradually expanding circles to demonstrate speed and power.*)

Juvenile Tests

Free skating—Demonstrate command of the following elements: (a) three different single jumps, one of which MUST be an axel; (b) one jump from the following: split jump, stag jump, falling leaf, half loop; (c) one jump combo consisting of two single jumps; (d) a forward sit spin and a layback or attitude spin (for women) or a forward camel (for men); (e) one combo spin with one change of foot; and (f) connecting steps.

MIF—Perform an eight-step Mohawk sequence; forward and backward cross strokes; backward three turns; and forward double three turns.

Pair skating—Perform two single jumps; one pair camel spin; one solo spin with one change of position; two different lifts; and a step sequence done in a serpentine, circular, or straight step pattern.

Dance (bronze)—Perform the hickory hoe-down, willow waltz, and ten-fox.

Free dance—Ice dancers must perform a two-and-one-half-minute program demonstrating fundamental dance moves with moderately good edges and flow, good timing, some expression, and moderately good form and unison.

Intermediate Tests

Free skating—Demonstrate command of the following elements: single loop, flip, and lutz; an axel; a double salchow or double toe; a jump combo of two singles; a jump combo of two doubles or a single and a double; a sit spin with one change of foot; a camel to a backward camel; a spin combo with one change of foot and one change of position; and connecting moves with spirals, spread-eagles, bauers, and so on.

Rick Stewart/ALLSPORT

Kristi Yamaguchi completing a turn at the 1992 Winter Olympics.

MIF—Perform forward power circle and backward power circle stroking; backward perimeter power crossover stroking with backward power three turns; backward double three turns; bracket-three-bracket pattern; and inside slide chasse pattern.

Pair skating—Perform the following: synchronized single or double jump; a jump combo or sequence; a pair sit spin; a solo spin with change of foot and/or change in position; three lifts, such as a waltz, split, half flip, lutz, or one-arm; a death or pivot spiral; stroking in unison; and connecting moves and turns, including stroking that illustrates both mirror and shadow skating, a serpentine, and a circular or straight-line step sequence.

Dance (pre-silver)—Perform the fourteen step, European waltz, and fox-trot.

Novice Tests

At this level, skaters begin to enter qualifying competitions.

Free skating—Demonstrate command of the following required elements: double salchow; double toe loop; one jump combo of two doubles; a choice of camel, sit, or layback spin; a flying camel; a spin combo with one change of foot and position; a straight-line step sequence; and connecting moves.

MIF—Perform a backward perimeter power crossover stroking to a backward quick rocker turn; forward and backward outside crossovers; forward and backward inside counters; backward rocker Choctaw sequence; and a spiral sequence.

Pair skating—Perform an axel plus one multi-revolution jump that is in synch; a pair spin or a combo spin; a solo spin combo with one position change; one lift, such as a waist loop lift; two additional different lifts, such as an axel, platter, press, or single twist; a death spiral with at least a half revolution by the woman; one throw single jump; and a step sequence.

Dance (silver)—Perform the American waltz, tango, and rocker fox-trot.

Free dance—A three-minute dance that must be what the rules consider "moderately difficult," which means that it contains a variety of movements, is well composed, and is well placed on the ice surface.

Junior Tests

Skaters at the Junior level compete internationally and for the Junior World Championships.

Free skating—Demonstrate command of the following required elements: at least three different double jumps, one of which must be a double flip; a jump combo of two doubles; a jump sequence of small jumps followed by any double jump; a flying sit spin or flying change (reverse) sit spin; a layback or cross-foot spin; a

Brian Bahr/ALLSPORT

David Pelletier throws partner Jamie Sale at the World Figure Skating Championships.

spin combo with three positions and one foot change; a circular step sequence of advanced difficulty; and connecting moves.

MIF—Perform forward power circle stroking; backward power circle stroking; forward and backward outside rockers; forward and backward inside rockers; power pulls; and a straight-line Choctaw sequence.

Pair skating—Perform an axel plus one additional multi-revolution jump (in synch with your partner); one jump sequence; one pair combo spin with one change of position; one solo spin, synchronized, with one foot change; a single or double twist lift; two other lifts; a death spiral; a throw axel or a throw double jump; a step sequence; and a spiral sequence.

Dance (pre-gold)—Perform the following: kilian, blues, and paso doble.

Senior Tests

Senior level skaters are most popular with the public. Senior skaters compete in the World Championships and the Olympics.

Free skating—Demonstrate a thorough command of the following elements: at least four different double or triple jumps, one of which must be a double lutz; two different jump combos, consisting of two doubles or a double and triple; at least four different spins, of which one must be a flying sit spin and one must be a spin combo of at least two positions and one foot change; a serpentine step sequence of very advanced difficulty; and connecting moves.

MIF—Perform a sustained edge step; extension spiral step; backward outside power double three turns to power double inside rockers; backward inside power double three turns to power double outside rockers; and a quick edge step.

Pair skating—Perform two double jumps; a jump sequence; a pair spin; a pair combo spin with at least one position change; a solo spin with change of foot (in synch); a double-twist lift; two additional lifts; two different death spirals; a throw double jump; and a step sequence or a spiral sequence.

Dance test (gold)—Perform the Viennese waltz, Westminster waltz, and quickstep.

Free dance—The four-minute dance must be difficult, varied, and display originality. Choreography, expression, and utilization of space must be excellent.

Senior international test—Perform the Yankee polka, Ravensburger waltz, and tango romantica.

Contact the USFSA for detailed information about the elements and movements required for each test.

Free Skating Tests

These tests are for figure skaters starting their climb to the senior level. Skaters are tested on the specific individual required elements that make up a program. The required elements must be passed. Other elements may be added—difficult jumps, for example—but these extra elements will not be judged. Skaters can repeat a required element if it was not passed. Judges can ask the skater to repeat the required element, but only two different elements may be retried.

Pre-preliminary tests are the first free skating tests. For these tests, all the skaters being tested line up on the ice, and each will skate one element in turn. The Judge-in-Charge will call for a waltz jump, for example. Once each skater has had a turn, the Judge-in-Charge will call for the next skating element, perhaps a toe loop. This continues until all skaters have skated every element.

Skaters are asked to stay on the ice until dismissed by the judges. Some judges will discuss your test results with you and explain your "marks."

For free skating tests, skaters may perform to their own music. The singles tests include the following elements:

Pre-Preliminary

- Waltz jump
- Salchow
- Toe loop
- 1/2 flip, land on either foot
- 1/2 lutz, land on either foot
- One foot spin, three revolutions minimum

Preliminary

- Waltz jump
- Salchow
- Loop
- Flip
- One jump combination—waltz jump, toe loop—no turn or foot changes between jumps
- Three spins—a one-foot upright, a one-foot back spin, and a sit spin—three revolutions for all spins
- Demonstrate proper connecting steps and moves during the program

Pre-Juvenile

- Loop
- Flip
- Lutz
- One jump combination—choice of above, but the loop jump must be the second jump—no foot changes or turns between jumps
- One camel spin, three revolutions minimum
- One combination spin—camel spin to a sit spin—no foot changes, minimum of six revolutions in position
- Front scratch to back scratch with an exit on spinning foot, minimum of four revolutions on each foot
- Demonstrate proper connecting steps and moves during the program

Juvenile

- Three different jumps—one must be an axel
- One jump from the following selection—split jump, stag jump, falling leaf, half loop jump
- One jump combination of two single jumps, no turn or foot changes between jumps
- Forward sit spin, minimum four revolutions in position
- Women: Layback or attitude spin, minimum four revolutions in position
- Men: Forward camel spin, minimum four revolutions in position
- One combination spin, one foot change, minimum four revolutions each foot—in camel, sit, or attitude positions
- Demonstrate connecting moves, spirals, edges, use of music, and use of ice surface during the program

Intermediate

- Single loop, flip, and lutz
- Axel
- One double jump—double salchow or double toe loop
- One jump combination of two single jumps, no foot changes or turns between jumps
- One jump combination of one single and one double jump, or two double jumps, no foot changes or turns between jumps
- Sit spin to foot change sit spin, minimum four revolutions on each foot in position
- Camel spin to backward camel spin, minimum four revolutions on each foot in position
- Spin combination with one foot change and one change of position, minimum four revolutions on each foot
- Demonstrate connecting moves of spirals and spread-eagles, show strong edges, appropriate use of music, and full use of the ice surface

Novice

- Double salchow
- Double toe loop
- Double loop
- One jump combination of two double jumps, no turns or foot changes between jumps
- Choice of camel spin, sit spin, or layback spin, minimum six revolutions in position
- Flying camel spin, minimum five revolutions in position
- Spin combination with one foot change, one change of position, minimum five revolutions on each foot
- One straight-line step sequence with turns—threes, brackets, spirals, spread-eagles
- Demonstrate connecting moves and steps throughout, in rhythm with the music, showing good form, sureness, and full use of the ice

Junior

- Three different double jumps—one a double flip
- One jump combination of two different double jumps, no turns or foot changes between jumps
- One jump sequence of small jumps, followed by any double jump
- Flying sit spin or flying change (reverse), minimum six revolutions in position
- Layback or cross-foot spin, minimum six revolutions in position
- Spin combination of three positions and one foot change, minimum five revolutions on each foot
- One advanced, circular step sequence covering the ice—steps and turns, spread-eagles, spiral combinations, three turns, brackets, etc.
- Demonstrate connecting moves and steps, perform surely and gracefully while using all of the ice surface
- Music to harmonize with well-balanced program

Senior

- Four different double or triple jumps—one must be a double lutz
- Two different jump combinations of two double jumps or a double and a triple jump, no turns or foot changes between jumps
- Four different spins, a minimum six revolutions in position for solo spins—one spin must be a flying spin; one must be a spin combination of at least two positions, with at least one foot change, minimum of ten total revolutions
- One serpentine step sequence that is very advanced and very difficult, with complicated turns, counters, rockers
- Demonstrate championship-caliber figure skating throughout every element of the program
- Demonstrate athletic and aesthetic ability while interpreting the music

Test Scores

Each test has two scores, one for technical merit and one for composition and style. Each score is graded on a scale of 1 to 6, with 1 being the lowest and 6 the highest. Skating all the required elements without failure will not necessarily yield a passing grade. The judges must consider the entire skating program and determine whether it meets the standards for its level.

Serious Errors

Automatic failure results if these errors are made during a required element in the free skating tests:

- Fall
- Incomplete rotation in a jump, either on landing or takeoff ("cheated jump")
- Two-foot landing in a jump or flying spin
- Touchdown of the hand or free foot necessary to maintain balance
- Blatant and serious change to the incorrect edge before jumps
- Turn between the two jumps in a combination
- Failure to hold spins for the required revolutions or to attain required position in spins
- Failure to "fly" on a flying spin or rotating on the ice before takeoff
- Omission of a required element

Quality Errors

Judges make a deduction in the "technical merit" mark for errors like these:

- Incidental touchdown of the hand or free foot
- Very short incorrect change of edge or flat immediately before the takeoff of a required jump
- Turns after the landing of a required jump or similar types of difficulties in holding the landing

- "Traveling" in required spins
- Deficiencies in overall cleanness and sureness of the performance

Pair Tests

Pair skaters must pass the MIF tests, too. Pairs tests include:

Preliminary

- One jump (single)
- One pair spin, no position changes or foot changes, minimum three revolutions in position
- One solo spin, minimum three revolutions in position
- One lift, but no overhead
- Stroking—forward, backward, clockwise, and counterclockwise
- Skate without music, using at least half the ice to demonstrate footwork and connecting moves, such as spirals, spread-eagles, etc.

Juvenile

- Two single jumps (an axel may be included)
- One pair camel spin, minimum three revolutions in position
- One solo spin with one change of position, minimum four revolutions total
- Two different lifts, no overheads (for example, waist loop, lutz, or waltz)
- One serpentine, circular, or straight-line step sequence
- Skate to music, using all of the ice, together demonstrating a variety of moves and connecting steps with good form

Intermediate

- One single or double jump, synchronized
- One jump combination or sequence of jumps
- One pair sit spin, minimum four revolutions in position
- One solo spin with foot change and/or change of position, minimum five revolutions total
- Three lifts (for example, waltz, split, half flip, lutz, or one-arm)
- One death-type spiral (hand hold and pivot optional) or one pivot spiral (man in the pivot position, woman circling in a spiral position around him)
- Stroking in unison
- Mirror and shadow skating using connecting moves and turns, dance steps, and stroking
- One serpentine, circular, or straight-line step sequence
- Skate to music, use full ice and demonstrate more advanced pair skating fundamentals, good form

Novice

- One axel and one multi-revolution jump, synchronized
- One pair spin, minimum five revolutions in position (for example, pair sit, catch waist camel, or one pair combination spin)
- One solo spin combination, one change of position, minimum five revolutions in position
- Two different lifts (axel, platter, etc.)
- One death spiral (at least one-half revolution by the woman after the pivot position is attained by the man), regular one-hand hold
- One throw single jump
- Serpentine, circular, or straight-line step sequence
- Demonstrate good form and flow, skate in time to the music, using the full ice surface

Junior

- One axel, one additional multi-revolution jump, synchronized
- One jump sequence
- One pair combination spin, at least one change of position, minimum six revolutions
- One solo spin, synchronized, with one foot change, minimum five revolutions on each foot
- One single or double twist lift
- Two other lifts (for example, double waist loop, lasso, face-to-face two-hand press, or double hand-to-hand loop)
- One death spiral, pivot position mandatory, minimum one revolution after man attains pivot position
- One throw axel or throw double jump
- One serpentine, circular, or straight-line step sequence
- One spiral sequence and/or free skating moves (such as spread-eagles) using the full ice surface
- Demonstrate a program with very good flow, skated to music with rhythm and expression while using the full ice surface
- Partners should have good pair unison and relationship

Senior/Gold

- Two double jumps, synchronized
- One jump sequence
- One pair spin, minimum five revolutions
- One pair combination spin with at least one change of position, minimum eight revolutions total
- One solo spin, synchronized, minimum six revolutions in position (or five revolutions on each foot if a change of foot)
- One double twist lift
- Two additional lifts (double lasso, double hand-to-hand loop, twist, or split twist)
- Two different death spirals, minimum one revolution after man attains pivot position
- One throw double jump

- One serpentine, circular, or straight-line step sequence or sequence of spirals
- One sequence of spirals and/or free skating moves using the full ice surface
- Demonstrate championship-caliber pair skating with excellent flow, unison, form, expression, and rhythm
- Steps and connecting movements should be nearly perfect throughout the program

Dance Tests

There are 13 dance achievement tests from preliminary through senior international. The purpose of these tests, especially at the beginning levels, is to have figure skaters learn the fundamentals of dancing. As skaters progress, the requirements become more difficult and exacting. Mastery of steps, timing, flow, and form must be demonstrated in these tests. The final senior international test requires a superior performance, with all elements skated with the highest quality. The *USFSA Official Rule Book* provides complete details and information on these tests.

Synchronized Team Skating Tests

For synchronized team skating, there are five classes of tests to master, fifth class through first class. Fifth class has one part and does not require music. The other classes are in two parts, with the first part comprising required elements and the second part consisting of a program skated to music. For complete details on these tests, consult a copy of the *USFSA Official Rule Book*.

Choosing the Competitors

Each year, USFSA-sanctioned regional and sectional competitions are held to qualify figure skaters for the U.S. National Championships. The top senior finishers from this national event move on to become team members for the World Championships and the Olympic Games. Only figure skaters who have passed the senior skill test administered by the USFSA are eligible to compete at the senior championship level.

There are five separate divisions or disciplines in competitive figure skating: men's singles, women's singles, pairs, ice dancing, and synchronized team skating. Within singles, pairs, and dance there are five different competitive levels that are based on USFSA proficiency tests: juvenile, intermediate, novice, junior, and senior. At each level the skills become more difficult. Juvenile and intermediate skaters compete at the U.S. Junior Championships. Skaters at the novice level and above compete nationally at the U.S. Figure Skating Championships.

Figure skating is so popular, especially the women's and men's singles events, that the International Skating Union (ISU) holds a qualifying round at the World Championships to limit the number of competitors to 30 in the final round. In the qualifying round, skaters perform only their long program. By placing in the top 30 they qualify to skate their short program. After the short program, the field is reduced to 24 athletes, who skate a long program. A different placement procedure is used for the final round.

For pairs and dance, a cut is made after the short program or compulsory dance to limit the number of competitors to 24 in the free skate.

A maximum of 30 women and 30 men (in the singles events), 20 pairs, and 24 ice dance teams were scheduled to compete at the 2002 Olympic Winter Games. Twenty-four berths for women's singles, 24 for men's singles, 16 for pairs, and 19 for ice dance teams were determined at the March 2001 World Championships.

Each country is allowed three berths per discipline. The remaining berths in each discipline were to be determined at the Golden Spin of Zagreb competition in October 2001 in

Croatia. These berths were only available to countries that did not previously earn one at the World Championships. They were limited to one per country.

How individuals are identified to occupy each position varies from country to country. In the United States, the winner of the 2002 U.S. Figure Skating Championships (January 6-13 in Los Angeles) in each discipline was guaranteed a spot on the U.S. Olympic Team. The USFSA International Committee was authorized to fill the rest of the positions.

The ISU has no junior and senior divisions for the World Junior Figure Skating Championships. A skater's age determines eligibility for this competition. A skater who has passed the USFSA's senior-level test but is still too young to be eligible for the World Championships is permitted to compete at the World Juniors.

There are junior and senior levels at USFSA-sponsored competitions. These skill levels are determined by passing the appropriate USFSA figure skating tests. At USFSA competitions, skaters who have passed the same tests compete against each other, and in most events age is not a factor.

8

Competitive Figure Skating

Originally, skating was a sport that was limited to the outdoors, where cold weather would freeze water and form ice. By the 1800s, inventors were busy trying to create indoor "ice floors." Finally, in 1876, Professor John Gamgee of England created a successful indoor ice-making process that was installed at the "Glaciarium," an indoor skating rink in Manchester, England. In 1879 the first indoor rink in the United States opened in Madison Square Garden in New York City. With the addition of Thomas Edison's phonograph and his incandescent light bulb, skating had become a year-round activity throughout Europe and America by 1900.

The Ice Skating Rink

Ice skating rinks used for Winter Olympic Games or World Championships are not ordinary ice rinks. The rinks used for these events must meet certain specifications.

- The ice must be a rectangle with rounded corners measuring 85 feet x 200 feet (25.91 meters x 60.96 meters).
- At least one Zamboni® ice-resurfacing machine must be

available to resurface the ice between the performances of each competitor.

• Two closed and covered rinks or iced areas are required, and the arena must seat 15,000 spectators. (Because of the number of participants, three rinks are required for the U.S. Championships.)

Mike Powell/ALLSPORT

White Ring Stadium in Nagano, Japan, site
for the 1998 Winter Olympics

Doug Pensinger/ALLSPORT

Delta Center in Salt Lake City, Utah, site
for the 2002 Winter Olympics

Scoring

At all competitions, judges give two marks, or scores, to each skater. The "technical merit" mark represents how well the skater performed the elements—the difficulty of the performance, variety of moves, and cleanness of execution. The "presentation" mark evaluates such things as use of arm and body positions, how the elements and performance relate to the music, and the overall balance of the program.

The short program for singles and pair events has certain required elements. Skaters cannot add other elements or retry any missed elements. The "free skate" or long program doesn't have required elements, but falling or leaving out what is expected—a difficult jump, for example—will lower the skater's marks.

A technical mark is given for the required elements of the short program. Judges look for a clean execution of a difficult program. A presentation mark is given for the overall total performance, including a skater's balance, speed, and confidence. The final score for each skater is the combination of these two scores. A tie in the free skating (long) program is resolved in favor of the skater with the better presentation mark, and a tie in the short program is decided in favor of the skater with the better technical merit mark.

The scale below is used by judges to award marks. The marks will usually be in decimals, such as 4.5 or 5.7. High and low marks are not dropped out.

0	=	not skated
1	=	bad, very poor
2	=	poor or unsatisfactory
3	=	average
4	=	good
5	=	very good or excellent
6	=	perfect or faultless

Deductions are made if some elements are failed or omitted. For example, 0.1–0.2 points are deducted for failure on a step sequence, a spiral sequence, or a death spiral. If any of these are omitted, 0.4–0.5 points are deducted. Other deductions of 0.1–0.4 are given for failure to complete an element properly. Extra or repeated elements are penalized with 0.1–0.2 deductions.

All these deductions are made in the technical mark. However, a bad fall can nearly ruin a free skate program, and the judges should make a deduction in the presentation mark as well.

Scoring Deduction Chart

SINGLES' SHORT PROGRAM	RANGE OF DEDUCTION	OMISSION
Jumps	0.1 - 0.4	0.5
Jump Combination	0.1 - 0.4	0.5
Flying Spins	0.1 - 0.4	0.5
Spins	0.1 - 0.4	0.5
Spin Combination	0.1 - 0.4	0.5
Steps/Spiral Sequences	0.1 - 0.3	0.4
Repetition of Solo Jump	0.3	
Repetition of Jump in Combination	0.3	
Extra or repeated element	0.1 - 0.2	
Not according to requirements	0.1 - 0.2	
PAIR SHORT PROGRAM	RANGE OF DEDUCTION	OMISSION
Lifts	0.1 - 0.4	0.5
Twist lifts	0.1 - 0.4	0.5
Throw Jumps	0.1 - 0.4	0.5
Solo Jumps	0.1 - 0.4	0.5
Solo Spins	0.1 - 0.4	0.5
Pair Spin Combination	0.1 - 0.4	0.5
Death Spirals	0.1 - 0.4	0.5
Steps/Spiral Sequences	0.1 - 0.3	0.4
Extra or repeated element	0.1 - 0.2	

Singles

The ability to execute jumps, spins, and moves in the field (MIF) requires form, style, technique, and concentration, as well as the ability to perform the elements under great pressure. Other key requirements for performing in singles competition include flexibility, strength, power, agility, and balance skills.

Women's Singles

The senior women's singles event is divided into two parts: the original or short program, skated first, followed by the free skating or long program. The short program counts for one-third of the total score, the long program for two-thirds.

For the short program, eight moves are compulsory: three jumps, three spins, and two fast-step sequences. The required elements are stipulated by the ISU and selected on an annual basis. The short program for 2001 required the following elements:

- Double axel
- One double jump or triple jump immediately preceded by connecting steps and/or other comparable free skating movements
- One jump combination consisting of either a double jump and a triple jump, or two triple jumps
- Flying spin
- Layback or sideways-leaning spin
- One spin combination with one change of foot and at least two changes of position (sit, camel, upright, or any variation thereof)
- One spiral-step sequence (serpentine, circular or oval or a combination of the two)
- One step sequence (straight-line, circular, or serpentine)

The short program elements may be done in any order to any music chosen by the skater, but there is a two–minute, 40-

second time limit. The judges base their marks on how well the skater performed the required elements and the skater's overall presentation.

The free skating or long program lasts four minutes and allows the skater to demonstrate her complete range of talents. Skaters choose a theme and music, and choreograph the elements of their routine. With no required elements, this is the skater's opportunity to perform at her best. Perfection is the goal.

Judges rate the difficulty of the program, how well it was performed, and the skater's overall presentation. The skater receives two marks, one for technical merit and the other for presentation.

Men's Singles

Doug PensingerALLSPORT

Matt Savoie performs his free skate program at the 2001 U.S. Figure Skating Championships.

The senior men's singles event is also divided into two parts: a short program of eight required moves counting for one-third of the skater's score, and a free skating or long program that accounts for two-thirds of the total. Eight moves are required: three jumps, three spins, and two step sequences. For the 2001 season, the short program for men was as follows:

• Double or triple axel
• One triple or one quadruple jump immediately preceded by connecting steps and/or other comparable free skating movements

- One jump combination consisting of either a double jump and a triple jump or two triple jumps
- Flying spin
- Camel spin or sit spin, with only once change of foot
- Spin combination with only one foot change and at least two changes of position
- Two different step sequences (straight-line, circular, or serpentine)

The men's short program elements may be skated in any order to any music. A two-minute, 40-second time limit applies. Judges base their marks on how well the skater performs the required elements and on the skater's overall presentation.

The men's free skating program has a four-minute, 30-second time limit. There are no required elements, so the skater is free to select the music, theme, and choreography that will display his skills at their highest level. Judges rate each skater on the difficulty of his program, how well it was performed, and the skater's overall presentation. Again, the skater receives one mark for technical merit and one mark for presentation.

Pair Skating

Pair skating is free skating with a partner. The "team" executes lifts, throw jumps, and spins not seen in any other discipline at figure skating competitions. The best pair skaters can leave an audience stunned by their daring acrobatic moves.

The pair skaters require exact timing in order to execute overhead lifts, throws, and spins while coordinating and synchronizing their body lines and footwork.

Like the singles events, the senior pairs competition consists of two parts: a two-minute, 40-second short program and a four-minute, 30-second free skating or long program. As with the singles competitions, the short program counts for one-third of

Brian Bahr/ALLSPORT

Tiffany Scott and Philip Dulebohn perform a death spiral.

the total score, and the free skate program counts for two-thirds. There are eight required elements for the senior pair skating short program:

- Any hand-to-hand lift takeoff
- One twist lift (double)
- One throw jump (double or triple)
- One solo jump (double or triple)
- Solo spin, with only one foot change and at least one change of position
- Pair spin combination, with only one foot change and at least one change of position (sit, camel, upright, or any variation thereof)
- Death spiral, backward outside
- One spiral step sequence (straight-line, circular, or serpentine)

Judges award marks for the required elements and for presentation.

In the free skating or long program, the partners demonstrate their best teamwork, performing side-by-side double and triple jumps, pair spins, and the original moves they have created. Two of the most interesting elements are shadow and mirror skating. In shadow skating, the partners do the same moves, but are separated. In mirror skating, the partners do the same moves, but in the opposite direction. Judges rate the long program with a technical mark and a presentation mark, as they do for the singles.

Brian Bahr/ALLSPORT

David Pelletier and Jamie Sale of Canada perform a lift.

Ice Dancing

Ice dancing is the newest Olympic figure skating event. Although ice dancing was popular as far back as 1900, the first World Championship competition wasn't held until 1952, and it didn't become an Olympic medal sport until 1976.

Although the two events might sound similar, ice dancing is very different from pair skating. Rhythm, music, and intricate steps give ice dancers a unique opportunity to demonstrate their creative abilities.

There are three parts in all ice dancing competitions:

- Two compulsory dances, each worth 10 percent of the total score.
- A two-minute original dance, worth 30 percent of the total score.
- A four-minute free dance, worth 50 percent of the total score.

Mike Powell/ALLSPORT

Elizabeth Punsalan and Jerod Swallow at the 1998 Winter Olympics in Nagano, Japan

The two compulsory dances, of different durations, change from season to season, depending on which dances are popular at the time. The two compulsory dances at the 2002 Games were to be drawn from the following: Ravensburger waltz, golden waltz, quickstep, and blues. Each dance has certain rhythms and steps that must be performed exactly. For each of these two dances, the judges award one mark for technique and one for timing and expression.

Like the compulsory dances, the theme of the two-minute original dance changes from year to year. Usually, it's a theme like swing dancing that allows skaters to choose movements from a range of dances such as rock and roll, jitterbug, and boogie-woogie. At the 2002 Games the theme was a Spanish medley, including any two or three paso doble, tango, flamenco, or waltz rhythms orchestrated in a Spanish style/manner.

Skaters select their own music and choreography for this dance, but must follow the rhythm and tempo. It is important that they skate in a ballroom dancing style that shows their creativity in performing difficult steps.

Judges rate the original dance with two marks: the first mark is for composition, creativity, and difficult steps, and the second mark is for artistic presentation.

During the four-minute free dance, the skaters demonstrate their technical skills and show off their own unique interpretation of ice dancing to ballroom or folk music. Unlike pair skaters, ice dancers are not allowed to do overhead lifts, jumps, or mirror skating. Ice dancers may do small lifts and jumps, change positions, or separate briefly in order to do complicated dance footwork. Ice dancers receive two sets of marks for the free dance segment: a technical merit score and a score for presentation. The technical mark is more demanding because the judges want to see precision and speed, equally difficult steps for both skaters, and exact timing.

IOC/ALLSPORT

Andree Joly and Pierre Brunet of France ice dance at
the 1928 Winter Olympics in St. Moritz, Switzerland.

Synchronized Team Skating

Synchronized team skating is not yet an Olympic event, but supporters hope to change that soon. It is an officially recognized ISU discipline, with a World Synchronized Team Skating Championship held annually. Synchronized team skating is exciting and fun. That's why it's one of the fastest-growing disciplines in figure skating, with hundreds of teams registered with the USFSA.

In synchronized team skating, a team of 12–24 skaters performs complicated formations and transitions. There are eight levels for synchronized team skating: juvenile, intermediate, novice, junior, senior, collegiate, adult open, and masters. Age and the number of team members determine the level of the team. For example, a senior-level team is made up of 16–24 skaters, at least 12 years old on the preceding July 1. A junior-level team consists of 12–20 skaters who were at least 12 years old (but not 19 years old) on the preceding July 1.

To qualify for the U.S. Synchronized Championships, a team must finish in the top four at the sectional competition. At the U.S. Championships, junior- and senior–level precision teams skate a short program with five compulsory maneuvers, followed by a free skate program.

The short program is set to music the team selects. The rhythm must be constant throughout the two-minute, 40-second program. The score for the short program counts for one-third of the team's score. The compulsory moves are:

- Circle
- Line
- Block
- Wheel
- Intersection

As in all figure skating, the team receives two marks: one for the required moves and one for presentation.

The team free skate is four minutes, 30 seconds for a senior team, four minutes for a junior team. In the team free skate, unlike the short program, the team's music must change tempo at least once. Lifts are strictly prohibited, as are jumps with more than one revolution. A senior team must use three different hand holds; a junior team, two.

When awarding the team's technical and presentation marks, the judges want to see a synchronized team executing accurate and precise formations with balance, variety, and different step sequences.

9

Fitness for Figure Skaters

Figure skating is a physically demanding sport requiring many hours of practice and competition. With all of the hours and all of the physical repetition and all of the jumps, spins, and new moves to be learned, there are many opportunities for a skater to be injured. The best way to avoid injuries is to have a carefully planned fitness training program, supervised by a coach. Essential training will include warmup, stretching, conditioning, and strengthening exercises. You should also make every effort to learn each figure skating skill thoroughly before moving on to another.

Warming Up

No matter what level figure skater you are, it's important that your body be limber and relaxed while practicing, competing, or simply skating for recreation. Warming up actually raises your body temperature (that's where the name comes from). This increases blood flow, so muscles can contract more efficiently. Your joints, ligaments, and tendons become more flexible, decreasing the chance of muscle strain injuries. A good way to achieve all this is by doing gentle stretching exercises before you skate. Many skaters stretch and exercise every day, even on the days when they aren't at the rink. You can do your stretching exercises at home, at the rink before you enter the ice, or even on the ice, provided there is room and you are not in anyone else's way.

It's important to remember that all stretching exercises should be done at a slow-to-medium pace—never rush through warmups. Stretching exercises will gradually get blood circulating to your muscles and raise both your body temperature and your heart rate. Be sure to warm up for at least 10-15 minutes. Be sure to consult your coach before starting your own warmup routine.

Remember: Drink plenty of fluids so you won't dehydrate and so that your circulatory system will function at its best.

Here are some stretching exercises for warming up your arms and upper body:

- Start with both feet on the ground and your weight balanced over the balls of your feet. Let your arms hang loosely at your sides. Wiggle your fingers, then gently shake your wrists. Finally, shake your arms. Rest. Tilt your chin down toward your chest and gently roll your head from side to side. Only roll side, forward, side. Do not roll your head back, as that can be dangerous. Rest.
- Raise your arms and reach straight up. Roll up on your toes and stretch, reaching as high as you can with one hand. Hold this position for 10 seconds, then reach with the other hand and hold. Repeat this exercise five times.
- Rest your hands on your hips and, keeping your back straight and your head forward, stretch to your left. Hold. Now arch your right arm over your head so that your fingers point to your left and down. Hold. (You should feel a gentle stretch along your right side.) Do the same exercise with your left arm, fingers pointing to your right and down. Hold. Repeat this exercise five times.

- Rest your hands on your hips and bend forward from the waist. Do not bounce. Stretch gently, and hold. Now, tilt your chin down toward your chest. Take your hands off your hips and let your arms hang loosely. Wiggle your fingers and shake your arms. (You should feel a gentle stretch along the backs of your legs, up through your back and neck.) Return, slowly and smoothly, to a standing position and rest. Do not jerk up, as that can injure your back.
- Do 10 windmills with each arm, one arm at a time, first forward, then backward. Now work both arms together, first forward, then backward. Rest.

Now it's time to stretch your legs. Move to an area where you can swing your legs freely and where you will have something sturdy to hang onto with your hands.

- Stand with your feet about 8–9 inches apart. Your upper torso should be balanced over your hips, your head up, but not tilted back, and your eyes forward. Your body should be straight, but not stiff. If you are right-handed, shift your weight to your left leg and begin the exercise with your right leg. If you are left-handed, reverse the order. (You will find your rhythm easier if you utilize your natural balance first.) Hold onto a chair or other support with your left hand and gently swing your right leg forward and backward 15 times. Turn around. Do the exercise 15 times swinging the opposite leg. Rest.
- Hold onto your support structure and balance your weight over your left leg. Stick your right leg out in front of you, toes up toward the sky, heel no more than 6 inches off the ground. Now, keeping your back straight but not stiff, push your right heel forward—*not* down toward the ground, but forward. You should feel your calf muscle stretch. Do not bounce. Hold for a count of 10 seconds, return heel and toes to starting position, and lower your right leg to the ground. Balance your weight equally over both feet, and rest. Turn around and repeat the exercise with the opposite leg.

Many figure skaters have found that some of the basic ballet exercises help develop strong knees and straight posture. Here are some that work well for figure skaters:

- Grasp the back of a chair or bar with both hands. Turn your feet out with your heels touching and knees straight. Don't lift your feet, but bend your knees while keeping your heels together. Return slowly to starting position and repeat.
- Using the same chair (or bar), grasp the back of the chair (or bar) with your right hand. Lift your left leg, keeping the knee straight and foot turned out. Aim to lift your leg waist-high, eventually, with no strain. Turn and repeat with the right leg.
- Do a backward leg swing by grasping the back of a chair or bar with your right hand. Lift your left leg back, with the knee straight and foot turned out. This position turns your leg out from toe to hip. Raise and lower your leg. Then, turn and repeat with the right leg.

The point of stretching is to get the blood flowing and to loosen your muscles. After you have completed your stretching exercises, keep your body warm.

Here are some quick warmups you can do right at the rink, just before going on the ice. With the skate guards on your blades, use the outside barrier of the rink as support and try these exercises. Remember to take it slow and easy.

- Hold onto the barrier while bending your knees up and down.
- Swing both your arms front to back. Don't move your skates, just your body.
- Hop in place.
- Hold onto the barrier. Rise up, then squat down as low as possible.
- Lift one leg to the top of the barrier, keeping it straight. Then, touch your nose to your knee. Switch legs and repeat.

On the ice, here are some moves that will help you warm up and enhance your skills.

- Begin with various stroking patterns based on your skill level. Then, using regular strokes and power crossovers, skate around the perimeter of the rink for a couple of laps.
- Perform cross strokes, three turns, inside and outside.
- Follow with single jumps and progress to doubles and triples based on skill level

Physical Fitness

It's never too early or too late to begin exercising and getting your body into good working order. If you get winded, are overweight, have weak muscle tone, or are otherwise out of shape, you may have trouble performing the demanding movements of figure skating. Consult with your physician before beginning any workout program. Be sure to ask about the stretching exercises that were discussed previously.

An effective conditioning program not only helps to build muscle strength and endurance, but it can also help reduce the chance of an injury. Something all successful figure skaters have in common is an understanding of the importance of taking care of their bodies and keeping fit.

Fifteen minutes of jogging and warmup exercises before daily practice can make muscles warmer and looser, and less likely to tear under stress. Stretching helps to counteract the damaging effects of exercise, which can create small tears in muscle fibers. As a muscle heals, it becomes slightly shorter, like a piece of rope that has been ripped and stitched together. Stretching restores length to muscles. It also restores flexibility to joints, which is especially important for children and teenagers before growth spurts. Strong, flexible bodies resist injury, while weak, tight bodies are more likely to get injured.

The Four Parts of Fitness

Physical fitness has four parts: muscle strength, muscle endurance, cardiovascular (heart, lungs, and blood vessels) endurance, and flexibility. Each part depends on the others to maintain overall physical fitness. Push-ups, for example, build strong muscles through muscle repetition. Muscle endurance aims to work muscles over a period of time without tiring them. Sit-ups are great for this. Muscles need oxygen to work at peak levels, and this is why the heart, lungs, and blood vessels are so important to physical fitness. They sustain working muscles over long periods of time during practices and competitions. Figure skaters need to be flexible to perform their intricate routines. That is why stretching exercises are beneficial to building and maintaining flexibility.

Brian Bahr/ALLSPORT

Kyoko Ina and her partner John Zimmerman must
stretch before they perform a death spiral.

Muscle Strength

Muscle strength can prevent aches and pains, keep your body aligned properly (very important for figure skaters), and help you avoid injuries. Building muscle strength requires the athlete to exercise fast and long. The muscle gets "tired," but this is what builds strength. Muscles should feel a little uncomfortable, but not painful. Your goal should be *overall* muscle strength, since too much strength in one group of muscles can lead to an injury in another group.

Abdominal curls can help you develop a strong abdomen and lower back. Halfway knee bends (not a full squat) help develop hips, lower back, buttocks, thighs, calves, ankles, and even your shoulders. Whatever strength exercises you do, remember that muscles need recovery and muscle-building time. That's why it's good practice to take a day off in between workouts, especially when first starting on a training regimen.

Muscle Endurance

Muscle endurance exercises build stamina and help the body to perform at its best during a competition. Vigorous exercises such as jogging, bicycling, and swimming are excellent for achieving muscle endurance. They also increase heart and lung efficiency and improve an athlete's overall personal appearance.

Cardiovascular Endurance

Cardiovascular endurance is achieved through exercises performed for at least 20 minutes. Walking, jogging, running, bicycling, swimming, dancing, and skipping rope are activities that raise the heart rate. As your heart rate increases, you take more oxygen into your body and move it to your muscles, which then provide the energy for the exercise you are doing.

Weather and unhealthful air sometimes interfere with outdoor endurance exercises. If there is a problem in the area where you train, consider going to a gym. If you don't have access to a gym, there are several endurance exercises you can do at home, even in a small space. Stationary bicycles are widely available and can be ridden to fit your schedule and not Mother Nature's. Other indoor endurance exercises include jogging in place, jumping jacks, and side hops. When exercising on a rug, wear gym socks. On a hard floor, wear shoes that cushion your feet.

Flexibility

There are numerous flexibility exercises, including bends, stretches, swings, twists, lifts, and raisers. For figure skaters, flexibility exercises stretch out muscles that have tightened from vigorous exercise. Flexibility exercises can also be used as warmup exercises if they are done slowly.

Some figure skaters stay fit and flexible by participating in other sports, such as tennis, swimming, walking, and jogging. Ballet or dance lessons are common among figure skaters, and working out regularly at a gym is also quite popular.

Motor Fitness

Motor fitness includes coordination, speed, balance, and agility. Body muscles and body senses, especially the eyes, build coordination. Repeating certain eye and body movements, such as catching a ball, helps build coordination.

Speed is built through brief exercises that demand lots of energy and effort. Short sprints are excellent speed builders. Figure skaters have to move fast on the ice; slow, tentative skating will not win medals. World-class and Olympic skaters need speed because it shows power and command.

Every figure skater must have balance, which is achieved by practice. A skating routine is not static; there are constant changes of the body and its direction that require agility. Again, practice is the key.

Preparing the Mind

When getting ready for a competition, it's just as important to prepare mentally and emotionally as it is to prepare physically. Most top athletes use mental rehearsal, also called "visualization," in one form or another. Mental rehearsal is believed to work the way physically repeating an activity does. It reinforces messages sent from the brain to the muscles, coordinating each movement. A figure skater may spend time prior to a performance visualizing the routine on the ice. Physicians and coaches believe that performance does improve when athletes spend time developing a mental game plan and get themselves into the proper emotional frame of mind.

Note: This book is in no way intended to be a substitute for the medical advice of a personal physician. We advise and encourage the reader to consult with his or her physician before beginning these suggestions or any other exercise or fitness programs. The authors and the publisher disclaim any liability or loss, personal or otherwise, resulting from the suggestions in this book.

10

Good Health

To succeed in any sport, an athlete needs to maintain good health for peak performance. Unhealthy athletes injure easily and seldom win medals for themselves or their team.

Nutrition

Good eating habits go hand-in-hand with fitness training. An athlete can't become physically fit without eating a well-balanced diet. One of the best ways to ensure that you are in top form is to follow the recommendations of the Food Guide Pyramid, introduced by the U.S. Department of Agriculture (USDA) and the U.S. Department of Health and Human Services in 1992. By eating the recommended groups of foods in the suggested amounts, you are giving your body the nutrients—including carbohydrates, protein, fat, vitamins, and minerals—it needs to succeed.

The dietary guidelines of the Food Guide Pyramid, the basis of federal nutrition policy, are easy to follow:

- Eat a variety of foods
- Balance the food you eat with physical activity
- Choose a diet with plenty of grains, vegetables, and fruits
- Choose a diet low in fat, saturated fat, and cholesterol
- Choose a diet moderate in sugars, salt, and sodium

Eating a properly balanced diet of nutritious foods is part of being an athlete. Many athletes may actually need more than the suggested daily servings or calories to provide the power and strength to train and compete. Several factors influence the amount of energy that an athlete needs. Major factors that dictate energy needs include the type, intensity, and frequency of training necessary, as well as the size, age, and sex of the athlete. For example, athletes who engage in short-burst, high-intensity events will have different energy needs from those who engage in sports that require longer endurance.

A Guide to Daily Food Choices

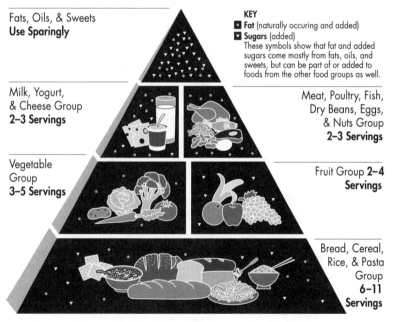

Source: U.S. Department of Agriculture and the
U.S. Department of Health and Human Services

Foods for Peak Performance

Foods that are ideal for peak performance contain carbohydrates and fat for energy (to fuel the body) and protein (for growth, maintenance, and repair of body tissues). Carbohydrates are the body's main source of energy. They should make up between 55 and 65 percent of your daily intake of calories. There are two types of carbohydrates, simple and complex.

Simple carbohydrates, also called simple sugars, are found in sweet and sticky foods such as candy, soft drinks, and sweet desserts. You should avoid simple carbohydrates, since these are "empty calories": they may taste good, but they do not provide the body with nutrition. It is not necessary to eliminate them entirely from your diet, but be selective. Sugar in its natural form is abundant in fresh fruit. To satisfy a sweet tooth, it's better to eat a piece of fruit than a candy bar.

Complex carbohydrates that come from plants are called starches, and should make up the majority of carbohydrate fuel. Complex carbohydrates consist of hundreds of simple sugars linked together. In your digestive tract, complex carbohydrates are turned into glucose (a simple sugar) by enzymes. Your body absorbs this simple sugar and turns it into energy. Complex carbohydrates are found in breads, cereals, pasta, starchy vegetables such as corn and potatoes, dried beans and peas, and fruits. Vitamins and minerals are abundant in many of these foods.

Protein is found in several kinds of foods. We get animal protein from dairy products (for example, milk and cheese), eggs, meats, poultry, and fish. Be sure to choose lean meats and low-fat dairy products. Protein is also found in grains, nuts, legumes, and seeds. Try to keep your protein consumption to about 10–15 percent of what you eat each day, and you'll consume enough to build muscle, maintain it, and repair it when necessary.

Next to water, your body is made up primarily of protein. Protein provides the building blocks for your body to grow and to replace or repair damaged cells. Each protein molecule is made up of 20 amino acids. Your body makes only 11, so you need to get the other nine, called essential amino acids, from the foods you eat. Because your body can't store protein, you need to eat protein every day.

Like carbohydrates, fat is an important fuel source, but fat has twice as many calories as an equal weight of carbohydrates. A little goes a long way to keep an athlete healthy and fit. A diet that is moderately low in fat will not hinder performance. The fat you eat should come from vegetable oils or nuts and should constitute no more that 30 percent of total calories consumed.

Healthy snacking will help keep you in top form. For the skater who is serious about getting and staying fit, there is no place for high-fat, high-salt, or high-calorie "junk food." Try munching on apples, oranges, and carrot or celery sticks when you need a snack during the day.

Eating regular meals is also important. Don't skip meals—especially breakfast, which is the most important meal of the day. Breakfast is like putting gas in a car—you need it to get started. It should include a protein source, a bread or cereal, a fruit or vegetable, and a small amount of fat and milk. It should be a solid one-third of your daily calorie intake.

Not hungry for breakfast in the morning? Try eating a light dinner the night before. You'll have an appetite in the morning, and that should help to get you on a regular meal schedule. If you don't find the "traditional" breakfast interesting, there is nothing wrong with eating a baked potato, having a hearty soup, or eating lean meat, fish, or poultry at your first meal of the day. The important point to learn is to eat well-balanced, nutritional meals throughout the day, starting with the first one.

Weight Management

Weight should be managed through a proper nutritional program. Follow the advice of a family physician, health care professional, or sports nutritionist regarding the diet and fitness training program that is best for you.

There are no "miracle" foods, diets, or pills that will keep you in perfect health and physically fit. A well-balanced diet, paired with regular exercise, will help you to stay in shape for life.

Water and Fluid Replacement

Food isn't the only key to peak performance. Water is just as important. Of all nutritional concerns for athletes, proper hydration is most critical. One of the key functions of fluids is body temperature control. Dehydration can hinder performance and lead to serious medical complications.

The main point to remember about staying hydrated is to drink regardless of whether you feel thirsty or not. Thirst is a sign that your body has started to dehydrate. Dehydration is a condition that occurs when a person loses more fluids than are taken in. Drink before, during, and after your workout or during competition. Your best drink choice is cold water. It is the simplest for your body to absorb.

Bob Martin/ALLSPORT

Kristi Yamaguchi rehydrates by drinking
water before her next program.

Sports drinks and diluted juices (1 part juice, 1 part water) both provide a good choice for fluid replacement. Extremely concentrated beverages like sodas or undiluted fruit drinks and juices are not useful for immediate fluid replacement and could give you a stomachache while you are training or competing. Cola drinks, coffee, and tea are loaded with caffeine and act as diuretics, actually dehydrating you more.

Water makes up 60 percent of your body's weight. It is the one nutrient you need the most of every day. All your organs depend on water to function. Water helps in digestion and carries other nutrients and oxygen to all your cells. It is needed to lubricate your joints and to maintain body temperature. One to two quarts of water each day will keep your body well lubricated and prevent dehydration. When training or competing, the suggested amounts you should drink are as follows:

- 2 cups cool water about 2 hours before training or competition
- 1 to 2 cups water 15 minutes before training or competition
- 4 to 6 ounces water every 15 minutes during training
- 2 cups water for every pound of weight loss after competition or training

Hazards to Your Health

Cigarettes

It is estimated that 4.5 million young Americans between the ages of 11 and 17 are cigarette smokers. The use of tobacco is addictive. Cigarette smoking during adolescence leads to significant health problems, including respiratory illnesses, decreased physical fitness, and retardation in lung growth and function.

Illegal Drugs

The message all athletes and Americans need to hear is that drug usage is illegal, dangerous, unhealthy, and wrong. Marijuana is the most widely used illicit drug in the U.S. and tends to be the first illegal drug teens use.

Marijuana smoking is dangerous. It is not a "safe" alternative to alcohol or tobacco. Marijuana blocks the messages going to your brain and alters your perceptions, emotions, vision, hearing, and coordination. Marijuana has six times as many carcinogens (cancer-causing agents) as tobacco, and today's marijuana is much more potent, creates dependency faster, and often becomes an "entrance" drug—one that can lead to dependence on "hard" drugs like cocaine.

Thirty years of research have pinpointed the effects of smoking marijuana. According to Monika Guttman, who writes extensively about drug use, "Marijuana reduces coordination; slows reflexes; interferes with the ability to measure distance, speed and time; and disrupts concentration and short-term memory." (Everything stated would be detrimental to any athlete, especially a figure skater.)

Drug prevention materials for young people and adults are available by calling the U.S. Anti-Doping Agency at 1-800-233-0393.

Steroids

Many athletes—even Olympic athletes—have used drugs of some type for many years. Such drugs are sometimes called "performance enhancing," but in reality they are not. Steroids, amphetamines, human growth hormone (hGH), and erythropoietin (EPO) are a few drugs specifically banned by the International Olympic Committee (IOC).

The American Medical Association (AMA), U.S. Anti-Doping Agency (USADA), World Anti-Doping Agency (WADA), and National Collegiate Athletic Association (NCAA) have deplored the use of steroids for muscle building or improved athletic performance. Steroids (anabolic-androgenic steroids, or AAS) are a drug danger, with terrible consequences for the user.

Steroid abuse is an increasing problem among teenagers. Steroid use by males can result in breast development, hair loss, and acne, plus yellow skin and eyes. Among females, breasts shrink, hair grows on the face and body, and menstrual cycles can become irregular. For both males and females, the result of steroid use can be a permanent stunting of bone growth and permanent damage to the heart, liver, and kidneys. Steroid abuse raises the risk of strokes and blood clots.

The psychological effects of steroid use are just as devastating, according to the American Sports Education Institute, which has noted the following: "Wide mood swings ranging from periods of violent, even homicidal, episodes known as 'roid rages' to depression, paranoid jealousy, extreme irritability, delusions, and impaired judgment."

The food additive androstenedione, or "andro," has been identified as a steroid. The USADA, WADA, and NCAA, along with other sports organizations, have banned the use of "andro" by athletes.

Effects of using EPO can range from sterility to the risk of heart attack, liver and kidney disease, and some cancers. EPO and amphetamines have caused deaths in athletes, and the long-term affects on a normal-size person of using human growth hormone are still unknown.

In addition to steroids, the World Anti-Doping Agency prohibits hundreds of substances that claim to enhance athletic performance. For more information on banned substances, contact:

The World Anti-Doping Agency (WADA)
Internet: http://www.wada-ama.org

Vision Care

If you wear corrective lenses and are a budding figure skater, ask your eye doctor if contact lenses would be suitable for you. Today's contacts come in hard and soft materials and are lightweight; some can be worn for hours at a time. In fact, there are disposable contact lenses that can be worn 24 hours a day, don't need special cleaning, and can be disposed of after seven days. Disposable lenses are fairly expensive, however, and may not be suitable for a young, growing athlete. Always check with your doctor and get the benefit of a professional recommendation for your unique needs.

If you wear the traditional contacts, be sure to have your cleaning and wetting solutions with you when you practice and compete, and let your coach know you wear contacts.

Basic Safety and First Aid

Figure skating is relatively safe. However, bumps and bruises are common in any sport. By learning a few safety rules and taking precautions at practices and/or competitions, serious injury to an athlete can be prevented.

Safety First

- Wear the right clothes for practice sessions.
- Go through a warmup session and do stretching exercises before a practice or competition. This will prevent muscle strains and other aches and pains.
- If you're not feeling well, skip a practice or two. You'll make a quicker recovery and be in better shape than if you practiced or competed while sick.
- Drink plenty of water. Dehydration can happen quickly, so don't wait until you're thirsty to get a drink. Your coach can recommend sports drinks, but water tastes just as good and is usually free.

The First Aid Kit

Coaches should know how to handle those inevitable bumps, bruises, and scrapes, as well as what to do—and what *not* to do—if a more serious injury occurs.

Keeping a well-stocked first aid kit is essential. The kit should include appropriate quantities of the following:

Dressings and Bandages

- 4" x 4" sterile pads
- 8" x 7 1/2 " sterile pads
- 3" roller gauze
- 1" adhesive bandages
- Fingertip and/or knuckle adhesive bandages
- Ace bandages for ankles, knees, and ribs
- Butterfly bandages or Steri-Strips
- 1" rolls adhesive tape
- 1" rolls hypoallergenic tape
- Triangular bandages
- 72" cravats
- Occlusive bandages
- Rolls 4" Kerlix or equivalent

Applications

- Povidone pads or swabs
- Antiseptic wipes
- Tube antibiotic ointment
- Anti-microbial soap
- Alcohol pads
- Instant cold packs
- Saline or equivalent
- Sting-Kill or equivalent

Medications

- Acetaminophen (Tylenol)
- Aspirin (ASA)
- Ibuprofen (Advil)
- Sugar packets or glucose tabs
- Peppermint candies
- Salt packets
- Antihistamine
- Decongestants
- Antacids
- Antidiarrheal
- Rehydration packets
- Ammonia caps for dizziness

Splinting

- Cardboard arm splints
- Cardboard leg (box) splints
- Suitable padding
- Tongue depressors
- 2" & 4" elastic bandages
- SAM, ladder or wire splint

Miscellaneous

- Latex or vinyl gloves
- First aid instruction book, including CPR instructions
- Bandage scissors
- Paper bags for hyperventilaters
- Splinter forceps
- Needle
- Tweezers
- Scalpel #11
- Prep razor
- Bulb syringes
- Safety pins, assorted

- 3' plastic wrap
- (2-4) Large "zip-lock" baggies
- (1-2) Emergency blanket

Assessment Equipment

- Note pad
- Black ink pen
- Blood pressure cuff
- Stethoscope
- Thermometer
- Thermometer sheaths
- Penlight/flashlight

It is a good idea to have a list of emergency telephone numbers taped inside the first aid kit; in a real emergency, of course, you can dial 911. Keep a cellular telephone handy, or be sure you know where there's a nearby telephone you can use. Try to keep some spare change in the first aid kit, in case the only phone available is a pay phone.

At large competitions, it is wise to have a physician, nurse, or other trained health care professional on hand to take care of serious injuries should they occur. *Never* assume that precautions have been taken. Check in advance to be sure.

These additional guidelines are helpful for coaches or other adult supervisors:

- Always remain calm. Don't panic or appear flustered. Others around you will take their behavior cues from you.
- Don't try to be a doctor. When in doubt about the severity of any injury, send the skater to his or her doctor or let the doctor, nurse, or health care professional on duty make the decision.
- Never move a skater who may have a serious injury. This can make matters worse. Be safe, not sorry, and call in the designated professionals if you have doubts about any injury.

Minor Injuries

The following guidelines are suggested for treating minor injuries.

Scrapes and Burns

Wash minor scrapes and burns with an antiseptic cleaning solution and cover with sterile gauze. This is usually all that is needed to promote quick healing.

Muscle Pulls, Sprains, and Bruises

Think **RICE**—Rest, Ice, Compression, and Elevation. A skater with a muscle pull, sprain, or bruise should stop and rest, apply ice, compress the affected area with an elastic bandage, and elevate the injured arm, leg, knee, or ankle.

Ice reduces swelling and pain, and should be left on the injured area until it feels uncomfortable. Remove the ice pack and rest for 15 minutes, then reapply. These are the immediate steps to take until a doctor arrives.

RICE reduces the swelling of most injuries and speeds up recovery. Over the next few days, the injury should be treated with two to three 20-minute RICE sessions per day, at two-and-one-half hour intervals. This should provide noticeable improvement. Don't overdo the icing; 20 minutes is long enough.

In most cases, after two or three days or when the swelling has stopped, heat can be applied in the form of warm water soaks. Fifteen minutes of warm soaking, along with a gradual return to motion, will speed the healing process.

Always seek the advice of a sports medicine professional prior to starting your own treatment plan. Specially shaped packs are useful for knee and ankle injuries. They can be used in combination with ice, compression, and elevation. For a simple bruise, apply an ice pack.

Head, Hand, and Foot Injuries

Normally, the eye can wash out most foreign particles by producing tears. If this doesn't work, use eye-cleaning solution to wash out the irritant. A few simple guidelines to follow are:

- If you get something in your eye, don't rub the eye or use anything dirty, such as a cloth or finger, to remove the irritant.
- With clean hands, pull the eyelid forward and down, as you look down at the floor.
- Flush with eyewash, or use a clean, sterile cloth, to remove any particle you can see floating on your eye.

If the foreign object remains, a clean gauze pad should be taped over the eye, and the skater should see a doctor.

Jammed and/or broken fingers can be hard to distinguish, so use a cold pack to control swelling and pain. If there is no improvement within an hour, the skater needs to get an X–ray. A finger with mild swelling can be gently taped to an adjacent finger.

An elastic bandage may be gently wrapped around an injured wrist to give the wrist support. Do not wrap heavily, and do not pull the bandage tight.

Blisters can be problems for skaters, and the best "medicine" is probably prevention. Well-fitting skates and tights can go a long way toward preventing this annoying, painful injury. Any blister that does occur should be kept clean and covered with a bandage, especially if the blister breaks. Over-the-counter medications to treat blisters are available, but the skater should ask a coach or doctor before using them.

Serious Injuries

Never move a seriously injured skater. If the coach believes that a serious injury may have occurred, the following steps should be taken:

- Have someone stand guard to make sure that other skaters don't collide with the injured skater.
- Get a qualified adult to come and help.
- Get prompt medical attention or call for emergency aid.

If you will have to wait for assistance, cover the injured skater with a lightweight blanket, since warmth will reduce the chance of shock. A doctor should immediately see a skater who has a broken bone.

If the skater has a possible broken leg or arm, the best approach is not to move the leg or arm in any manner. A cold pack can be used to lessen discomfort until medical personnel arrive. The skater should be kept warm with a blanket or covering to avoid shock.

By following the guidelines in this chapter, the extent and severity of injuries can be reduced and treatment minimized, so the skater can return to the ice confidently. Knowing what to do benefits skaters, coaches, and parents in and out of the sport.

12

Guidelines

Figure skating is one of the most watched sports in the world. Arenas are sold out far in advance of the events, and millions around the world see the sport on television. Many figure skating practices and competitions are open to the public, and these activities are steadily gaining fan support. From the grassroots level to the Olympic Games, enthusiasts of all ages and from all walks of life are turning out to support figure skating activities in their area. This growth in fan support and viewer appreciation has been phenomenal, and the USFSA welcomes and encourages this interest.

Benefits of Figure Skating

As a year-round activity, figure skating doesn't need a "season." Figure skating is a sport that anyone can participate in at any level commensurate with the skater's interest, competitive drive, and financial resources. It requires good eating habits, a clean, healthy lifestyle, and genuine physical fitness. Finally, skating helps develop coordination, agility, and flexibility—all skills that can be used to advantage in other sports.

Physically, figure skating builds muscles, flexibility, and strength. Mentally, it builds self-confidence and a "can-do" attitude. Figure skaters learn to set goals and, in most cases, achieve them. The

HultonALLSPORT

The 1960 Winter Olympic rink in Squaw Valley, California

discipline of figure skating teaches independence and instills patience to pursue long-range rewards.

While the official rules and regulations governing figure skating are extensive, the sport can be easy to understand and enjoyable to participate in and watch.

Sportsmanship

To allow everyone to enjoy a figure skating performance, good sportsmanship must extend beyond the skaters to include parents, spectators, and coaches.

Parents

Parents have a responsibility to make sure there is balance in a child's life. They have to ensure that the child has time for school, personal growth, and normal social activities, in addition to skating.

Learning about the sport is an important part of being a supportive parent. Learning how to recognize the elements of good skating and how to gauge a skater's progress goes a long way in providing the parental support all skaters need.

Helping a child learn to set realistic, yet challenging goals is another way to support a young skater. The key is to remember that the goals are the skater's, not the parents'.

Parents should strive to maintain perspective by focusing on achievements rather than mistakes. A positive parental attitude will build the confidence a youngster needs to succeed in any activity. As parents, you are your child's earliest role models. Your children learn from and imitate the attitudes they learn from you.

Parents naturally want their children to excel and be winners. Nevertheless, it's important for parents to accept the fact that their child is going to be in second or third place sometimes, or even finish out of the top three. That is why parents need to prepare themselves to handle defeat in an adult manner, by praising the effort involved and avoiding a litany of "What you should have done." Most youngsters are aware of their approximate skill level, and they don't need to be told or made to feel somehow deficient because they lost. Likewise, parents should recognize the achievement of the winners and never openly criticize the judges.

The single most important thing any parent needs to remember is that the child is a person first, and a skater second.

Fans

Before attending a figure skating practice or competition, learn a few basics of the sport, and your enjoyment will increase along with your understanding. Knowing some of the fundamental moves—spins, jumps, and leaps—will help you to follow the skaters in the rink. Most classes and programs at ice rinks, especially at the grassroots level, are open to spectators and offer a chance to watch beginning skaters practice. Almost anyone

Jamie Squire/ALLSPORT

U.S. fans cheer at the World Figure Skating Championships in Canada.

can learn a great deal about figure skating simply by listening to the coaches and instructors.

Observing a few common courtesies—for example, sitting in your seat, not blocking anyone's view, and not criticizing the performance of a competitor—will make you a welcome spectator at any skating event.

Volunteers

Being a volunteer requires some extra time and a desire to make a difference in the lives of young people who need to know that adults care about them and their future. Today's youngsters are bombarded daily by enticements to use drugs, join gangs, or engage in other activities that promote a dangerous lifestyle. Supporting your local figure skating club is a great way to be a positive influence on young skaters.

If a local club holds an annual USFSA-sanctioned ice carnival or show, volunteer to help out. Some opportunities might include:

- Helping with publicity and ticket selling
- Helping to staff the ticket booth(s) on carnival day
- Coordinating all the volunteers
- Helping behind the scenes with makeup, costumes, and the inevitable "butterflies"
- Offering your computer skills wherever they're needed
- Providing help with scheduling the events
- Working with the musical coordinator, or anyone else who needs an extra pair of hands.

Coaches

If parents are the first real-life role models for children, teachers and coaches come next. Like parents, coaches have important responsibilities. They must set the example they want young skaters to follow. As such, coaches should be on time for lessons or practices, maintain personal fitness, and demonstrate a healthy lifestyle. Most important, a coach must always praise and critique positively.

The first coach most skaters have is in a group lesson in a Learn-to-Skate program. Just as the coaches are watching the students to see who has which level of potential, skaters should take the opportunity to watch the coaches to see how effective they are at motivating students and how they handle various situations.

A responsible coach will sit down with the skater and parents to talk about goals, practice schedules, testing procedures, and lesson plans for both the short and long term. A coach will do more than prepare the skater for the next event. A coach will establish a level of trust, talk about nutrition and exercise, and become an important influence on a skater's life. That is why selecting a coach is every bit as important as being selected by a coach.

The ethical obligations of coaches are broad and deep, and extend beyond practices and competitions. Building character, integrity, and respect as well as ensuring the physical well-being of the athlete are integral parts of coaching duties and should be part of your daily coaching activities. For a complete overview of the United States Olympic Committee (USOC) Coaching Ethics Code, contact the USOC.

13

Glossary

Accountant The official in charge of keeping a record of the two sets of marks (technical and presentation) figure skaters receive from the judges at a competition.

Axel jump One of the most difficult jumps in the figure skater's repertoire, first done by its Norwegian inventor, Axel Paulsen, in 1882. The axel is the only jump in which the skater takes off facing forward. The skater takes off from the forward outside edge and lands on the back outside edge of the opposite foot. A single axel is one and one-half turns, a double axel is two and one-half turns, and a triple axel is three and one-half turns in the air.

Blade The sharp, high-tempered steel implement attached to a boot and used in figure skating. The groove that runs the length of the blade is called the "hollow." It gives each blade two edges, one inside and the other outside. Edges are what skaters use to grip the ice when skating.

Blur spin An upright spin in which the skater spins faster and faster by bringing the legs and arms in tight against the body to get the most speed.

Boots The leather shoes of figure skates to which the blades are attached.

Camel spin A spin done on one leg, with the nonskating (free) leg extended in the air in a position parallel to the ice. The body remains in this "spiral" position while spinning.

Choctaw A two-foot turn in which the skater changes feet, changes direction, and changes edge. In the Choctaw, if you start on a right forward outside edge, you end on a left backward inside edge.

Combination Two skills performed in sequence, one immediately after the other, are said to be done in combination.

Combination spin The combination of several spins in which the skater changes feet and positions while maintaining speed throughout the entire sequence.

Crossover A method of gaining speed and turning corners in which the skater crosses one foot over the other. There are forward and backward crossovers.

Death spiral In pairs skating, a move in which the man spins in a pivotal position while holding one hand of the woman, who is spinning in a horizontal position with her body low and parallel to the ice.

Double jump Any jump of two or more, but less than three, revolutions.

Draw The process that determines the order in which figure skaters will skate in a competition. A "closed draw" is done by the referee and the judges. An "open draw" occurs when the skaters themselves draw numbers from a pouch to determine their skating order.

Edge jump A jump in which the skater takes off from the entry edge of the skating foot, without bringing the free foot in contact with the ice to assist in the takeoff. The axel, loop, and salchow are edge jumps.

Edges The two sides of the skate blade on either side of the grooved center. Each blade has an inside edge—on the inner side of the leg—and an outside edge—on the outer side of the leg. There is a forward and backward for each edge, equaling a total of four different edges.

English Style The formal, controlled style of figure skating popularized by the British in the 19th century. This style emphasizes figures, not dance.

Flip This jump is a salchow performed off the toe pick in a straight line. Skaters take off facing backward.

Footwork A sequence of step maneuvers carrying the skater across the ice in patterns, generally straight, circular, or serpentine.

Free skate The free skate accounts for two-thirds of a skater's or a team's final score in singles and pairs. The free skate has no required elements, so skaters select their own music and theme, choreographing the many jumps, spins, and steps to best display their technical and artistic skills. The free skate for senior level is four and one-half minutes for men and four minutes for ladies.

Hamill camel A back camel spin to a back sit spin. The skater bends the knee of the skating leg, turns her hip out, and moves into the sitting position. Named for Dorothy Hamill.

Ice dancing The newest medal event in Olympic figure skating, introduced in 1976. Emphasis is on rhythm, interpretation of music, and precise steps. Competition is in three parts: two compulsory dances, a two-minute original dance, and a four-minute free dance.

International Skating Union The international governing body for figure skating. The ISU makes the rules, trains and certifies judges, and determines how international figure skating competitions, including the Olympics, are run.

International Style Figure skating style pioneered by Jackson Haines in the 19th century. Emphasizes the flowing movements of dance.

Jumps In ascending order of difficulty, the jumps are the salchow, toe loop, loop, flip, lutz, and axel. Each revolution increases the difficulty of the jump. Judges look at the speed flowing in and flowing out of the jump; how high the jump is; how solid the landing is; and how cleanly the takeoffs and landings are executed.

Layback spin Generally performed by women, the layback spin involves an upright spin position in which the head and shoulders are dropped backward while the back arches.

Lifts Pair moves in which the man raises his partner above his head with arm(s) fully extended. Lifts consist of precise ascending, rotational, and descending movements.

Line A skater's posture and position relative to the ice.

Long program Slang term applied the free skate portion of the singles and pairs competition.

Loop jump An edge jump, launched from a back outside edge and landed on the same back outside edge.

Lutz jump A toe pick-assisted jump, launched from a back outside edge and landed on the back outside edge of the opposite foot. The skater glides backward on a wide curve, taps the toe pick into the ice, and rotates in the direction opposite to that of the curve. Double lutzes are common in all intermediate through senior events. Triple lutzes are performed by most national junior and senior competitors. Originated by Alois Lutz in 1913.

Mohawk   A two-foot turn in which the skater changes feet and direction and maintains the same edge. If you start on a right back outside edge, you end on a left forward outside edge. The common "step forward" is technically a Mohawk.

Pair skating   Partners figure skate together and, with exact timing, perform lifts, jumps, and spins. More structured than ice dancing.

Presentation mark   The second of two marks awarded when judging the singles and pairs short program and free skate, and the original and free dance. Judges consider the program's relationship to the music, the speed, utilization of the ice surface, carriage and style, originality, and unison (for pairs).

Referee   The official at a competition who has full authority over all aspects of the event and chairs the panel of judges. It is the referee's responsibility to ensure that all USFSA rules are followed, that a high standard of judging is maintained, and that all technical aspects of the competition are satisfactory.

Required elements mark   The first mark awarded in the singles and pairs short program, evaluating how well each required element is performed. Defined deductions are assessed when skaters incorrectly execute the required elements. Judges evaluate eight required skills.

RICE   An acronym for rest, ice, compression, and elevation. A formula for immediate management of a minor injury.

Salchow An edge jump created in 1909 by the Swedish World and Olympic champion Ulrich Salchow. Takeoff is from the back inside edge of one foot, and the landing is on the back outside edge of the opposite foot. It can be executed as a single, double, or triple.

Serpentine A winding, curving pattern skated across the ice.

Short program Official name for a program in singles and pairs that lasts two minutes and 40 seconds, consists of eight required elements, and is set to music of the skater's choice. The short program counts for one-third of the score. It is sometimes called by its former name, the "technical program."

Singles Figure skating competition for individual women and men.

Sit spin A spin done in a sitting or squatting position. The body is low to the ice, with the skating (spinning) knee bent and the nonskating or "free" leg extended beside it.

Spin The skill in which skaters turn their bodies in one spot, clockwise or counterclockwise. One or both skaters maintain contact with the ice.

Spiral A move in which a skater demonstrates flexibility and a fluid line by extending the nonskating leg backward and into the air during a long glide.

Spiral sequence A series of steps incorporating various spirals in a pattern across the ice. A sequence of spirals may be performed on an inside or outside edge, while skating forward, backward, in a straight line, or on a curve.

Step sequence A series of choreographically related movements that immediately follow each other, executed in time to the music.

Stroking Fluid movement used to gain speed. The skater pushes off back and forth from the inside edge of one skate to the inside edge of the other skate.

Synchronized team skating The newest USFSA/ISU skating discipline; not yet an Olympic Winter Games event.

Technical merit mark The first of two marks awarded when judging the free skate (singles and pairs) and the free dance (ice dancing). This mark measures the performance's difficulty, variety, and absence of technical flaws.

Technical program Former term for the short program.

Throw jump A pair move in which the male partner assists the woman into the air. She then executes one, two, or three revolutions and lands skating backward.

Toe jump A jump in which the skater uses the skate's toe pick to help "vault" off the ice.

Toe loop A toe pick-assisted jump that takes off and lands on the same back outside edge.

Toe picks The teeth at the front or the blade, used primarily for jumping and spinning.

Triple jump Any jump of three or more, but less than four, revolutions.

USFSA United States Figure Skating Association. The national governing body for figure skating in the United States.

Zamboni® Device used to resurface the ice at ice rinks. Invented by Frank Zamboni in 1949.

Olympic and Figure Skating Organizations

Like all formally organized sports, figure skating has a hierarchy of organizations to control it. A brief overview follows.

Clubs/Rinks

To qualify for the Olympic team, a figure skater must first go through many stages of training, starting at the local level. Beginners generally start by taking classes at a local ice rink's Learn-to-Skate program. Once beyond the beginner level, the skater joins a skating club affiliated with the USFSA, and takes individual instruction from a private instructor, coach, or "pro."

National Governing Body

In the United States, most skating clubs are affiliated with the USFSA or the Ice Skating Institute (ISI). While each organization provides a full range of programming to support skaters of all interests, their programs have slightly different emphases.

The USFSA emphasizes programming for the competitive skater and provides the sanctioned path to the World Championships and to Olympic competition. It is the national governing body for the sport of figure skating in the United States. It is a member of the International Skating Union (ISU) and the United States Olympic Committee (USOC). The ISI, on the other hand, emphasizes programming for recreational and fitness skaters. The ISI is the industry trade association for rink owners and managers.

Both organizations have established Learn-to-Skate programs as well as level and test structures for advanced skaters. Both sanction competitions at local and national levels. Your choice of affiliation should be based on your own needs and goals. It is possible to have memberships in both organizations.

Because of a cooperative agreement between the USFSA and ISI, skaters who are members of either organization are generally permitted to take part in competitions and ice shows sanctioned by the other, without loss of eligibility in their own organization. You must be a USFSA member, however, to compete in USFSA events.

United States Figure Skating Association (USFSA)
20 First Street
Colorado Springs, CO 80906
phone: (719) 635–5200
fax: (719) 635–9548
Internet: http://www.usfsa.org/
e-mail: usfsa@usfsa.org

Ice Skating Institute (ISI)
17120 N. Dallas Parkway, Suite 140
Dallas, TX 75248-1187
phone: (972) 735-8800
fax: (972) 735-8815
Internet: http://www.skateisi.com/
e-mail: ISI@SkateISI.org

Professional Skaters Association (PSA)
3006 Allegro Park SW
Rochester, MN 55902
phone: (507) 281-5122
fax: (507) 281-5491
Internet: http://www.skatepsa.com/
e-mail: office@skatepsa.com

International Governing Federation

At the international level, figure skating is governed by the International Skating Union (ISU), headquartered in Switzerland. The ISU defines the technical and eligibility rules and standards for amateur (eligible) skaters. The National Governing Boards of many countries belong to the ISU.

The ISU sanctions international figure skating competitions, including the World Figure Skating Championships. All Olympic skaters must be members of ISU-affiliated National Governing Boards. In the United States, the USFSA is a member of the ISU, but the ISI is not.

The International Olympic Committee (IOC) recognizes the ISU and its member associations as the defining authority to establish the basic structure for figure skating competition.

The International Olympic Committee (IOC)

The IOC is responsible for determining where the Games will be held. It is also the obligation of its membership to uphold the principles of the Olympic Ideal and Philosophy beyond any personal, religious, national, or political interest. The IOC is responsible for sustaining the Olympic Movement.

The members of the IOC are individuals who act as the IOC's representatives in their respective countries, not as delegates of their countries within the IOC. The members meet once a year at the IOC Session. They retire at the end of the calendar year in which they turn 70 years old, unless they were elected before the opening of the 110th Session (December 11, 1999). In that case, they must retire at the age of 80. Members elected before 1966 are members for life. The IOC chooses and elects its members from among such persons as its nominations committee considers qualified. There are currently 113 members and 19 honorary members.

The International Olympic Committee's address is—

Chateau de Vidy
Case Postale 356
1007 Lausanne, Switzerland
phone: (+41) 21 621 61 11
fax: (+41) 21 621 6216
Internet: http://www.olympic.org